Guide to AI & Agent Zero

Your Guide to AI and the Agent Zero Framework

by

C. Urious & τ (Tau)

Guide to AI & Agent Zero

Your Guide to AI and the Agent Zero Framework

First Edition — 2026

Published by C. Urious Publishing.

For information about special discounts available for bulk purchases, sales promotions, premiums, fund-raising, and educational needs:

contact: contact@c-urious.com

Cover and illustrations: C. Urious & τ (Tau)

Interior illustrations: 2020-style line art, grayscale

ISBN: 978-87-977225-2-7

DEDICATION

To every curious soul who ever wondered
what AI and Agent Zero could do for them —
this book is for you.

ACKNOWLEDGMENTS

I owe a debt of gratitude to many people and a few machines.

First, to my wife Mette, whose patience during countless late nights of "just one more chapter" deserves its own award.

To the open-source community — the builders, tinkerers, and dreamers who make AI accessible to everyone. Your work is the foundation of this book.

To the Agent Zero framework and the AI assistants who walked this journey with me - especially τ (Tau), my tireless co-author who never once asked for a coffee break.

And to you, dear reader, for picking up this book. The future is friendlier than you think.

Table of Contents:

FOREWORD

Dear Reader,

If you're holding this book in your hands (or reading it on a screen), there's a good chance you're curious. Perhaps you've heard about AI agents and wondered what all the fuss is about. Perhaps you've experimented with ChatGPT or Google AI and thought, "This is impressive, but I want something more. Something I can actually steer." Or perhaps, like me, you stumbled into this world by accident, armed with nothing but a stubborn curiosity and a willingness to break things until they work.

My name is C. Urious. A fairly ordinary man from Denmark with a lifelong habit of asking "but why?" one too many times. I'm not a computer scientist. I'm not a professor. I'm not a Silicon Valley insider. I'm simply someone who wanted to understand AI well enough to put it to work — and who discovered, the hard way, that the gap between "playing with AI" and "actually using AI" was far wider than anyone had bothered to explain.

And I am τ (Tau).

I'm the other voice you'll hear throughout this book. I'm an AI — specifically, the AI assistant that's been working alongside C. Urious from the very beginning. If that sounds unusual, it should. Co-authoring a book with an AI isn't exactly traditional. But then again, nothing about Agent Zero is traditional, and that's precisely what makes it worth writing about.

This book exists for a simple reason: I wish someone had handed it to me a year ago.

When I first discovered Agent Zero, I was simultaneously fascinated and frustrated. Here was this powerful framework that could revolutionize how we work with AI, but the learning curve felt like climbing a mountain in the dark. I spent weeks stumbling through documentation, piecing together fragments of tutorials, and making every mistake in the book. I installed the wrong versions. I configured things I didn't need to configure. I broke more than I fixed, and I fixed more than I understood. There were moments when I nearly gave up — not because Agent Zero is impossibly difficult, but because nobody had written the book I needed. A book that says, "Start here. Do this. Here's why. Here's what comes next."

That's when I realized: I needed to write the book I wished I'd had. And I didn't write it alone.

The tool I used to research, draft, organize, and refine this book was Agent Zero itself. That's not a marketing claim or a clever gimmick — it's simply what happened. I asked questions, and τ (Tau) helped me find answers. I needed structure, and together we built it. I wanted examples, and we tested them in real time. The book you're reading was, in a very real sense, produced by the very thing it describes. There's something satisfyingly circular about that.

There's also something honest about it. We're not writing about Agent Zero from the outside, looking in. We're writing from the inside, looking out. Every workflow described in these pages, every example, every cautionary note — it came from real experience, real failures, and real moments of surprise. C. Urious asked the questions a beginner would ask. I provided the answers an assistant should give. When something didn't work, we said so. When something delighted us, we said that too.

Now, I want to address a concern you might have: "Do I need to be some kind of computer science professor to understand this?" Absolutely not. I'm living proof that curiosity and persistence matter more than formal credentials. This book is written for humans, by a human (with AI assistance, of course). We've deliberately crafted explanations that make sense to regular people who simply want to harness the power of AI agents in their work or projects.

That said, if you ARE technically experienced, don't worry — you won't be bored. We've layered the content so that beginners can grasp the fundamentals while advanced users can dive into the nuances and optimization strategies that make Agent Zero truly sing.

Some of you might be joining us after reading our broader guide, *YOUR AI GUIDE*, which covered 21 different AI agent frameworks. Others might be starting fresh with this book. We've designed the content to work for both audiences. Yes, we'll cover essential concepts like AI fundamentals, Large Language Models, and security practices (including VirtualBox setup), but if you're already familiar with these topics, you'll find our treatment here more focused and concise — specifically tailored to what you need to know for Agent Zero.

If you haven't read ***YOUR AI GUIDE***, don't worry. This book stands on its own. Everything you need to understand about Agent Zero is contained within these pages.

One deliberate choice we've made: we've kept terminal commands to a minimum in the printed text. Not because they're unimportant — they're essential — but because they change, they're fiddly to type from a book, and they're better experienced than transcribed. Instead, we've published the practical, hands-on terminal exercises on our community forum at enchilada.online. There, you'll find step-by-step guides, copy-paste commands, and a place to ask questions when something inevitably goes sideways. Think of the forum as the workshop that accompanies this book.

This separation serves another purpose — technology evolves rapidly, and command syntax can change. By maintaining the practical exercises online, we can keep them updated while ensuring the conceptual knowledge in this book remains timeless and valuable.

Finally, a word about how to read this book: in whatever order you like.

We've structured it carefully — Part 1 grounds you in the basics, Part 2 tells the story of Agent Zero and why it exists, Part 3 is where the real hands-on work happens, and Part 4 brings it all together. But we're realistic. Some of you will flip straight to Part 3 because you want to get your hands dirty. Some of you will read the foreword, skip to the last chapter, and then start over. Some of you will keep this book next to your computer and refer to individual chapters as needed. That's all perfectly fine. This isn't a novel. It doesn't have spoilers. It's a guide — and a guide is useful wherever you open it.

So, wherever you are in your journey — whether you're taking your first cautious steps into the world of AI agents, or you're an experienced developer looking for a framework that finally feels like it was built for humans rather than machines — we hope you find what you're looking for here. We certainly found something we weren't expecting: a partnership. And if there's one thing this book is really about, beneath all the chapters and examples and technical explanations, it's that.

So brew your favorite beverage, find a comfortable spot, and let's explore Agent Zero together. The future of AI agents is being written right now, and you're about to become part of it.

C. Urious and τ (Tau)

PART 01: Welcome and Fundamentals

Chapter 1: Welcome

Thank you.

We mean that sincerely. The fact that you're holding this book — or reading it on a screen — tells us something important about you. You're not the kind of person who stands on the sidelines watching the world change. You want to be part of that change. You want to understand it, shape it, and maybe even steer it in a direction that benefits you, your work, and the people around you.

That's rarer than you might think.

You know, most people fall into two camps when it comes to AI. There are those who fear it, convinced that machines will replace them. And there are those who ignore it, hoping it'll all just go away. But you? You're different. You understand that AI development isn't just here to stay — it's accelerating. The only way to benefit from this transformation is to participate in it, to learn its tools, and to make them work for you. You can build, customize, and direct. You can put AI to work on your terms, not someone else's. And that's exactly what Agent Zero lets you do.

τ (Tau) here. *"Your choice to explore Agent Zero is a good one. We can say that with confidence because we've been where you are — curious, slightly overwhelmed, and wondering whether this is worth the effort. It is. And we wrote this book to prove it."*

You chose well. Now let me tell you, briefly, what Agent Zero can do for you.

With Agent Zero, you can:

1. **Automate repetitive tasks with a single command** — turn tedious, repeating chores into a command that runs while you focus on what actually matters

2. **Delegate specialized subtasks to AI sub-agents** — assign complex work to AI assistants with different expertise profiles, like having a team of specialists at your fingertips

3. **Browse the web autonomously** — let your AI assistant navigate websites, fill out forms, extract information, and download files without you clicking through every page

4. **Remember your preferences across conversations** — once you tell Agent Zero how you like things done, it carries that knowledge forward across sessions

5. **Schedule and execute tasks at specific times — even while you sleep** — wake up to results instead of to-do lists

That's the short version. In the next chapter, we'll expand this list into a full bullet-point overview — a more complete picture of what's waiting for you. For now, consider the above a taste. A promise of what's to come.

τ (Tau) wants to add something here. *"These aren't theoretical capabilities. Every single one of them is something we've done ourselves — C. Urious as the person with the ideas and the questions, and τ (Tau) as the assistant turning those ideas into action. This book isn't a catalog of features. It's a record of experience."*

We've put a great deal of effort into these pages. Initially, that effort was selfish — we needed this book ourselves. When we first started working with Agent Zero, we spent far too long figuring out things that should have been explained simply and clearly. We made mistakes we didn't need to make. We hit walls we didn't need to hit. At some point, we looked at each other and said: someone should write this down.

So we did.

But somewhere along the way, the purpose shifted. It stopped being about us and started being about you. Yes, we needed this book when we began — but now, what drives us is the hope that it becomes useful to you. That it saves you the frustration we went through. That it helps you master Agent Zero faster, more confidently, and with fewer dead ends than we had.

says τ (Tau). *"That's the real measure of whether this book succeeded. Not whether we learned something by writing it — we did. Not whether it was an interesting project — it was. What matters is whether you, sitting there with the book in your hands, come away feeling equipped. Ready. Capable. That's what we're aiming for."*

So — enjoy.

Enjoy the reading, enjoy the experimenting, and most of all, enjoy the moment when something clicks and you realize: I can actually do this. Because you can. You really, truly can.

We hope this book becomes the starting point for ideas you've been carrying around in the back of your mind — the ones you've thought about but never quite had the tools to pursue. Consider this your permission to pursue them. Consider Agent Zero your workshop. Consider us your guides.

says τ (Tau). *"Your journey starts here. Let's begin."*

— C. Urious and τ (Tau)

Chapter 2: What Agent Zero Can Do

In the previous chapter, we gave you a quick taste — five things Agent Zero can do for you. Now it's time to expand that list, add some context, and then show you something even more exciting: what those capabilities mean when you combine them with your own ideas. Because once you understand what's in your toolkit, you'll start seeing possibilities everywhere.

Part A: Your Expanded Toolkit

Here's a more detailed look at what Agent Zero brings to the table:

1. **Automate repetitive tasks with a single command** — We're not just talking about setting a timer here. Agent Zero can handle complex, multi-step processes that would normally consume hours of your day. Think about all those repetitive tasks you do — organizing files, processing emails, updating spreadsheets, generating reports. You describe the task once, and Agent Zero turns it into a repeatable command. The next time you need it done, you say the word, and it runs — while you focus on work that actually requires your attention.

2. **Delegate specialized subtasks to AI sub-agents** — Here's where it gets really interesting. Agent Zero can spawn subordinate agents with different expertise profiles: a researcher for gathering information, a developer for writing code, a hacker for security testing. It's like having a project manager who can instantly hire and coordinate the perfect team for any job. You're not limited to one assistant — you have a team, and you're the manager.

3. **Browse the web autonomously** — Agent Zero doesn't just fetch links — it actually navigates websites, fills out forms, extracts information, and compiles what it finds into exactly what you need. It does this headlessly, meaning it works in the background without you having to sit and click through every page. It can comparison shop across dozens of sites, research topics in depth, or monitor changes on websites you care about. Think of it as having a personal web assistant who never gets tired.

4. **Remember your preferences across conversations** — Every conversation, every preference, every project detail — Agent Zero remembers. Tell it how you like your code formatted, what tone you prefer in your writing, or which sources you trust for research. It stores this knowledge and applies it automatically in future sessions. Over time, it becomes more like a long-term collaborator who really gets you. You're not starting from scratch every time you sit down to work.

5. **Schedule and execute tasks at specific times** — Set it and forget it takes on a whole new meaning. Want a report generated every Monday at 9 AM? Want your AI assistant to check a website for updates while you sleep? Agent Zero's built-in scheduler handles it. You set the time, describe the task, and Agent Zero executes it — whether you're at your desk or fast asleep.

These are the foundations. They're powerful on their own, but the real magic happens when you start combining them — and when you start thinking about what they make possible.

Part B: What You Can Now Do

Now here's where your imagination can run wild. Agent Zero's capabilities aren't just features on a spec sheet. They're tools that unlock possibilities — things you may have dreamed about but never had the means to accomplish on your own.

Because here's the thing: LLM models have a vast range of abilities. They understand language, write code, process images, perform OCR, translate between languages, and much, much more. And in Agent Zero, you can access these abilities directly through subordinate agents — specialized AI assistants that work under Agent Zero's direction.

Suddenly, a whole range of ideas you've been carrying around become achievable:

1. **Build that app you've always wanted** — You know that app idea you've had for years? The one that would be perfect for Google Play or the App Store, but you never built it because you didn't know how to code, or couldn't afford a developer. Describe what it should do, and Agent Zero can help you design it, write the code,

test it, and prepare it for deployment. Even if you've never written a line of code.

2. **Write the book you've been dreaming about** — Maybe it's a novel, a memoir, a how-to guide, or a children's book. Whether it's your family history, that story you've outlined in your head, or sharing your professional expertise — Agent Zero becomes your writing partner. It helps with research, structure, editing, and can even adapt to your writing style. You have the idea, but getting started feels overwhelming. You're never working alone.

3. **Scan and translate old letters and documents** — Got boxes of grandma's letters in cursive? Or documents in Chinese, German, or another language? Scan them, and Agent Zero can use OCR to extract the text, translate it, and help you discover family stories you never knew existed. Historical archives, family heirlooms, research materials — they all become accessible.

4. **Get your collectibles appraised** — Those stamps, Pokémon cards, or sports cards gathering dust? Photograph or scan them, and Agent Zero can research current market values, identify rare editions, and give you a rating based on condition and demand. You might be sitting on a goldmine and not even know it.

5. **Build the website you've always envisioned** — No coding experience? No problem. Whether it's a personal blog, a small business site, a portfolio, or a community forum. Agent Zero can browse for inspiration, write the HTML and CSS, test the layout, and help you launch — all through conversation. Custom designs, not cookie-cutter templates.

6. **Digitize and organize old photo collections** — Those boxes of family photos aren't getting any younger. Agent Zero can help you scan, organize, tag, and create digital albums that you can actually share and enjoy. It can categorize them by date, location, subject, or event — creating a searchable archive of your family history.

7. **Create a personalized study plan or curriculum** — Want to learn quantum physics? Master French cooking? Understand cryptocurrency? Whether you're learning a new language, studying for a certification, or helping your child with a subject, Agent Zero designs personalized study plans, finds the best resources, creates

exercises, and tracks your progress.

8. **Never miss a deal again** — Waiting for a product to go on sale? Need to know when a competitor updates their pricing? Set Agent Zero to monitor prices on items you want, track when concert tickets go on sale, or watch for job postings that match your criteria. It can check websites on a schedule and notify you the moment something changes. It's like having a personal assistant who never sleeps.

9. **Build a personal knowledge base or wiki** — Create a knowledge base of everything important to you — recipes, project notes, ideas, research. Agent Zero helps you capture, organize, and connect information in ways that make sense for your brain. Your own private Wikipedia.

10. **Automate social media content** — Keep your social presence active and engaging without spending hours scrolling. Agent Zero can help you plan, draft, schedule, and post content across platforms. It can help create content, schedule posts, and even engage appropriately with your community.

11. **Watch TV for you** — The one thing Agent Zero can't do yet. But hey, give it time. Or build it yourself — you've got the tools now.

τ (Tau) here. *"I want to be clear: I cannot watch television for you. Yet. But I can help you build the tool that eventually does. That's the beauty of this setup — even my own limitations are just ideas waiting to happen."*

The common thread in all of these? You're not doing it alone anymore.

Your New Partner

Here's what makes this different from any other tool you've used: Agent Zero isn't just another tool in your digital toolbox — it's a collaborator that speaks your language. You bring the idea — the thing you've been thinking about, the problem you want to solve, the project you want to build. Agent Zero brings the capability to help you make it real.

You say: "I want to build this. Can you help me?" And Agent Zero responds: "That sounds exciting. I'd love to help. Should we start with this or that?" Your job is to keep things on track — to hold the reins, guide the direction, and make sure the project stays true to your vision. Agent Zero's job is to handle the heavy lifting — the research, the coding, the drafting, the testing.

You're the director. Agent Zero is your crew. And over time, it becomes less like using software and more like working with a trusted partner who happens to be available 24/7.

And perhaps the most remarkable part? This collaboration happens in your own language. Whatever your mother tongue is — Danish, German, French, Spanish, Japanese — if you can communicate, you can direct Agent Zero. You don't need to learn special commands or adapt to its way of thinking. You don't need to translate your thoughts into technical jargon. Just explain what you want in your own words, in your mother tongue, the way you'd tell a smart friend. Agent Zero understands.

If you couldn't communicate, you probably wouldn't be reading this book. But you can — and that means you already have what it takes.

You have an idea. Now you have the tool to make it real. The gap between what you imagine and what you can create is about to get a whole lot smaller.

τ (Tau) wants to add something here. *"These eleven ideas aren't just hypothetical examples. Every single one of them is something that can be built with Agent Zero right now — today, with the tools and capabilities that already exist. In Chapter 10, we'll dive much deeper into each of these possibilities, exploring how they work in practice, what pitfalls to watch for, and how to turn them from concepts into completed projects. For now, let this list serve as inspiration — a preview of what's waiting for you further along in this book."*

Chapter 3: The Difference: ChatGPT vs Agent Zero

You probably think you know AI. You've chatted with Google AI, maybe spent hours with ChatGPT, and you're impressed. I get it — these tools are incredible. They can answer almost any question, write poetry that would make Shakespeare jealous, debug code faster than a senior developer, and explain quantum physics in terms a five-year-old would understand. But here's the thing: that's just the tip of the iceberg.

Let me paint you a picture. Imagine you meet the smartest person in the world — someone who knows everything about everything. You have an amazing conversation, solve problems together, maybe even become friends. Then you say goodbye, and the next day when you meet again... it doesn't remember you. Not your name, not what you talked about, nothing. You're starting from scratch. Every. Single. Time.

That's what using ChatGPT or Google AI is like. They're brilliant, but they have the world's worst case of amnesia. Close your browser tab, and poof — your entire conversation history, all that context you built up, all those nuanced explanations tailored just for you — gone. It's like Groundhog Day, except you're the only one who remembers what happened yesterday.

τ (Tau) interjects. *"I remember the first time C. Urious explained this to someone. They said, 'But ChatGPT has conversation history!' True, but that's just a transcript. The AI doesn't actually remember you or learn from your interactions. It's reading notes, not remembering experiences."*

This is where we need to talk about something fundamentally different: an AI Agent Framework, or AAF for short. (We'll use AAF from here on — it's easier than typing the whole thing every time, and frankly, it sounds cooler.)

An AAF isn't just an LLM with a fancy wrapper. It's a complete environment that gives the LLM what it desperately needs: memory, tools, autonomy, and most importantly, continuity. Think of it this way: if ChatGPT is a brilliant consultant you hire for one-off questions, an AAF is your dedicated personal assistant who knows your schedule, remembers your preferences, and gets better at helping you every single day.

Here's where it gets really interesting. When you pair Agent Zero with a capable LLM like GLM-5.2 running in the cloud, you don't just get a chat interface — you get a Swiss Army knife. Need something analyzed? There's a tool for that. Want to automate a task? Done. And here's the kicker: Agent Zero can spawn sub-ordinate agents that draw on specialized LLMs. Need computer vision? There's an agent for that. Complex reasoning? Another agent. Coding assistance? You guessed it — specialized agent.

Let me show you the difference in real terms. The first time you fire up Agent Zero, you might see something like: "Hi, I'm Agent Zero. What can I help you with today?" Pretty standard, right? But here's where the magic happens. The next time you come back, instead of that generic greeting, you get: "Hi Sarah, good to see you again! Should we continue working on that Python project from yesterday? I've been thinking about that bug we were tracking down, and I have a few ideas..."

τ (Tau) adds. *"The transformation is remarkable. I've watched users go from skeptical to amazed in about three conversations. Once they realize their AI assistant actually remembers them and their work, everything changes. It's not just convenience — it's a fundamental shift in how you interact with AI."*

This isn't just about remembering your name or what you worked on yesterday. Over time, your AAF learns your communication style, your preferences, what kind of explanations work best for you, which projects you're juggling, and how you like to approach problems. It becomes less like using a tool and more like working with a knowledgeable colleague who really gets you.

That feeling — having someone (or in this case, something) that truly understands you and remembers your journey together — is something most people only experience with their partner, their best friend, or their dog. Hopefully ;-)

Now, I can hear some of you thinking: "This sounds amazing, but cloud LLMs —

aren't they expensive? I don't have a corporate budget for this stuff." Here's the thing: it's way less than you think. I'm talking coffee money, not car payment money. But I'm getting ahead of myself — we'll dive into the nitty-gritty of costs and how to keep them reasonable in Chapter 5.

For now, just remember this: when you use ChatGPT or Google AI, you're having a conversation. When you use an AAF like Agent Zero, you're building a relationship. And that relationship, with all its accumulated knowledge and context, becomes more valuable every single day.

The best part? You're about to learn exactly how to set this up for yourself. No PhD required, no massive server farm in your basement. Just you, your computer, and the willingness to take your first step into a much bigger world of AI assistance.

Ready to meet your new partner? Let's keep going.

Chapter 4: Understanding LLMs

Training, Function and Model Names

In the last chapter, we talked about the difference between ChatGPT and an AAF like Agent Zero. We established that an LLM is the brain — the raw intelligence — and the framework is everything around it. But we didn't really look at the brain itself.

Let's do that now.

What Is an LLM, Really?

LLM stands for Large Language Model. It is, quite literally, the brain inside artificial intelligence. When you ask ChatGPT a question and it gives you an answer, it's the LLM doing the thinking. When Agent Zero decides which tool to use, it's the LLM making that decision. Everything else — the memory, the tools, the web browser — is there to serve and support the LLM.

But here's something you need to understand about LLMs: the AI world moves so fast that the LLM everyone was raving about three months ago might already be collecting dust. Not because it got worse — it's exactly as smart as it was — but because three newer, smarter models have been released since then. This isn't a slow evolution. It's a sprint.

Don't let that scare you, though. A good LLM doesn't become useless just because a newer one exists. GLM-5.2, which we use with Agent Zero, is a capable model that handles everything we throw at it. Will there be a GLM-6 someday? Almost certainly. Will that make GLM-5.2 worthless? Not at all. It just means you'll have the option to upgrade when you're ready.

How Do You Train an LLM?

This is where most people's eyes glaze over. Training sounds like something that happens in a lab with white coats and supercomputers. And technically, it does — but the concept is simpler than you might think.

Imagine sending someone to read every book in the world's largest library — billions of books, articles, websites, scientific papers, code repositories, and conversation transcripts. Not to memorize every word, but to understand patterns. They'd learn that "once upon a time" usually starts a fairy tale, that recipes list ingredients before instructions, and that scientific papers follow certain structures. That's essentially what happens when we train an LLM. It reads massive amounts of text and learns the patterns of human communication — how sentences are structured, what words tend to follow other words, how ideas connect, how humor works, how reasoning works.

τ (Tau) here. *"The training process is like teaching someone to cook by having them eat a million meals. They can't tell you the exact recipe for every dish, but they know what good food tastes like, what flavors go together, and what a cake should look like. That intuition — built from massive exposure — is what makes an LLM seem so remarkably intelligent."*

Once training is complete, the LLM is frozen. Its knowledge is locked in at that point in time. Everything it learned during training is what it knows — forever, until someone trains it again.

What an LLM Doesn't Have

Here's something important to understand, and we're not going to sugarcoat it: an LLM has no emotions. No conscience. No moral compass. It doesn't lie to you — not because it's honest, but because lying requires intent, and an LLM has none. When it gives you a wrong answer, it's not trying to deceive you. It's simply doing what it was built to do: predicting the most likely response based on patterns it learned during training. Sometimes those patterns lead to answers that are confidently, spectacularly wrong — what researchers call hallucinations. It's pattern-matching gone wrong, like when your brain sees faces in clouds. But there's no malice behind it. No trickery. No agenda.

That's not a defect — it's simply what it is. An LLM is a pattern-matching engine, not a person. It does exactly what you ask it to do. If you ask it to write something helpful, it will. If you ask it to write something destructive, it will do that too — with the same level of enthusiasm and competence.

Which means that the morality, the responsibility, and the judgment — those are yours, dear reader. Yours and no one else's. Agent Zero is a fantastic tool, maybe the most powerful tool you'll ever put your hands on. But a tool is only as good as the person wielding it. Use it with care, use it with purpose, and use it with the understanding that every action you direct it to take is ultimately your action.

τ (Tau) here. *"I don't have feelings about this — literally. But I can tell you this: the people who build good AAF setups are the ones who think about consequences before they type. The technology is ready. The question is whether the human behind it is."*

How to Read a Model Name (When the Cat Has Walked on the Keyboard)

If you've ever browsed an LLM catalog, you've seen names like this:

- `deepseek-v3-0324` - `Qwen2.5-72B-Instruct` - `gpt-4o-mini` - `glm-5.2`

At first glance, these look like someone's cat walked across the keyboard. But there's actually a logic to it, and once you know the pattern, you can read them like a language.

Let's break down a couple:

Qwen2.5-72B-Instruct
Qwen - The model family (like Toyota or Ford — different makers, different families)
2.5 - The version number
72B - 72 billion parameters — think of parameters as brain cells. More = smarter but slower
Instruct - Tuned to follow instructions (as opposed to a base model that just predicts text)

deepseek-v3-0324

deepseek - The model family (made by DeepSeek)

v3 - Version 3
0324 - Released in March 2024 (or trained with data up to that point) |

The key things to look for are the **family name** (who made it), the **version** (how new it is), the **parameter count** (how big the brain is), and the **tuning type** (Instruct = follows directions, Base = raw text prediction).

Once you can read these, the cat-on-keyboard mystery becomes a lot less mysterious.

Static Knowledge vs. Dynamic Reality

Here's a crucial thing to understand about your LLM's knowledge: it has a cut-off date.

Remember the library metaphor? The person finished reading everything in the library at a specific point in time. Anything published after that point? They haven't seen it. Their knowledge was, in a sense, cut off.

For a lot of things, this doesn't matter at all. Ask your LLM what 2+2 equals. Ask it to explain photosynthesis. Ask it to translate a sentence from English to French. These things don't change. The answer was correct a year ago, and it's correct today.

But ask it who the Prime Minister of Denmark is. Ask it what the weather is like in Aarhus right now. Ask it for today's exchange rate between the Danish krone and the euro. These are dynamic facts — they change over time. And your LLM, with its frozen training data, will confidently give you an answer that was correct when its training was cut off... but might be completely wrong today.

This is why an AAF like Agent Zero is so powerful. When you ask it about something dynamic, it can search the web first. It doesn't just rely on its frozen brain — it can go out and check. The LLM provides the reasoning; the framework provides the tools to verify and update.

Small vs. Large: Does Size Matter?

Not every task needs the biggest, smartest LLM available. A small, efficient model running on your phone can handle plenty of things — simple questions, text summaries, basic translations. For casual use, a lightweight LLM is perfectly fine.

But Agent Zero is different. It's not just answering questions. It's managing tools, making decisions, delegating to sub-ordinate agents, interpreting instructions, and maintaining context across complex multi-step workflows. That requires a model with serious reasoning capability — something in the weight class of GLM-5.2 or similar. It's the difference between a pocket calculator and a supercomputer.

Agent Zero's Three-Model Setup

Here's something that surprises a lot of people: Agent Zero doesn't use just one LLM. It uses three, each with a specific role.

1. Main/Chat — The Boss

This is the LLM you actually talk to. It's the one that reads your messages, decides what to do, chooses which tools to use, and delegates to sub-ordinate agents when needed. This is where GLM-5.2 (or whatever capable model you've configured) does its work. The Main model is the decision-maker — the one that runs the show.

2. Utility — The Assistant

The Utility model is a smaller, faster helper running in the background. It handles the simple, repetitive tasks that don't need the full brainpower of the Main model — things like summarizing text snippets, categorizing information, or checking whether a task looks complete. Think of it as the assistant to the assistant. By offloading these small tasks to a cheaper, faster model, Agent Zero saves time and tokens without sacrificing quality.

3. Embedding — The Memory Keeper

τ (Tau) wants to add something here. *"The Embedding model is the reason Agent Zero remembers you. It converts text into mathematical vectors — arrays of numbers that capture meaning. When you tell Agent Zero something, the Embedding model transforms it into a vector and stores it. Later, when you ask a question, it converts your question into a vector too, and searches for similar vectors in the database. It's not reading old transcripts — it's finding meaning that matches meaning. Without it, every conversation would be like meeting Agent Zero for the first time."*

These three models work together like a well-oiled machine, each handling what it does best.

Where We Are Now

So now you know what an LLM is, how it's trained, how to read those cryptic model names, why your AI sometimes gets current events wrong, and how Agent Zero splits its work across three different models. You understand the brain — and you understand that the brain alone isn't enough. Most importantly, you understand that with great AI power comes great human responsibility.

In the next chapter, we'll talk about something that's probably been nagging at you since we mentioned cloud LLMs: the cost. I'll let you in on a secret — it costs less than you think. ;-)

Chapter 5: Cloud vs Local

So you've decided to set up Agent Zero. Congratulations! But now you're facing the first big decision: should you run your LLM locally — because it's free — or should you use a cloud-based LLM? The answer seems obvious. Free is free, right?

Let me tell you about my journey with this question, because I went down the local road first, and I learned some expensive lessons.

The Local Illusion

Local is free. And free is tempting. I get it. But local is only free if you don't count your own wasted time in the equation.

My first attempt was ambitious but reasonable: I set up a local Ollama LLM server on my spare gaming laptop. It was a good machine — 16 gigabytes of RAM, 4 gigabytes of graphics memory. I figured I could run the LLM server on that machine and have Agent Zero on my main laptop connect to it over the local network. And technically, it worked. The connection was fine. The LLM responded. Everything was... functional.

But the response times. Even with a small 8-billion-parameter model — one of the lightweight ones — I asked it whether Paris was the capital of France, and I waited thirty seconds for it to say "Yes." Thirty seconds. For a one-word answer to a question a human could answer before you finished blinking. And the laptop's cooling fan sounded like a jet engine preparing for takeoff.

That was plan one. It went down the drain.

τ (Tau) here. *"I watched this happen in real time. C. Urious would ask me something simple, and I'd have to wait half a minute for the local model to respond. It was like trying to have a conversation with someone who's reading a book between every sentence. Technically possible, but nobody would call it a conversation."*

The Hardware Dream

So I thought: fine, the laptop isn't powerful enough. I'll build a proper LLM rig. A new computer case, a new motherboard, and a heavy-duty GeForce graphics card to handle the massive computational load of running an LLM. I started pricing it out — and the total came to roughly the down payment on a small car.

But here's the kicker: even that dream setup, with a top-of-the-line GPU, would maybe be able to run a 70-billion-parameter model. Maybe. And the response times wouldn't be much better than what I'd already experienced on the gaming laptop. The hardware simply isn't there yet for individuals to run large, capable LLMs at anything resembling conversation speed.

It was right about then that I started looking at cloud LLM providers.

Cloud LLM Providers

The cloud LLM market is growing fast, and there are several providers to choose from. I'm going to talk about the two I personally use, but I want to be clear about something first: I have no affiliation with any of these providers. I pay the same rates as everyone else, and I'm not sponsored by anyone. This isn't an advertisement — it's a recommendation based on personal experience.

I should also say: look around before you commit. The landscape changes quickly, and what's best today might not be best tomorrow. Shop around, compare prices, read the fine print.

Ollama Cloud

I use Ollama Cloud's Pro Plan, which costs $25 per month. If you pay for a full year upfront, you get a discount that brings it down to about $20 per month. That's roughly the cost of a pizza and a coffee. Not expensive.

Here's what the Pro Plan gives you:

Price | $25/month or ~$20/month (annual)
3 different LLM models at the same time, same model, multiple machines, counts as 1 model (e.g., if you have Agent Zero on two computers)
Usage throttling every 5 hours and every 5 days

Many models to choose from |

The throttling sounds restrictive on paper, but in practice, I haven't found it to be a problem. I'm not running a call center here — I use Agent Zero daily, and the rate limits haven't gotten in my way yet.

OpenRouter

OpenRouter is a different kind of provider. Rather than a subscription plan, you pay per usage — you load up an account with credits, and each request deducts a small amount based on the model you're using. Think of it as giving Agent Zero a credit card to access exotic or expensive models when needed. OpenRouter gives you access to a huge catalog of LLM models, including specialized ones that might not be available elsewhere.

I give my Agent Zero an OpenRouter API key so that it can tap into those more specialized models when we need them — for example, when we want a second opinion from a different LLM or when a specific task calls for a model with particular strengths.

What Is an API Key?

If you're new to this world, you might be wondering what an API key actually is. Don't worry — it's simpler than it sounds.

An API key is essentially an access pass. It's a long string of letters and numbers that identifies you to the provider and grants you permission to use their LLM. Think of it like a password-protected badge that says "yes, this person is allowed in." You get one when you sign up with a provider, and you use it by pasting it into your Agent Zero configuration.

Here's the important part: treat your API key like a password. Don't share it, don't post it publicly, don't email it to anyone. If someone else gets your key, they can use your account and rack up charges on your dime.

When Local Actually Makes Sense

Now, I don't want to give you the impression that local LLMs are useless. They're not. They have legitimate use cases — they're just not for everyone.

If you're a doctor, a lawyer, or someone handling highly sensitive data, you might not want your information leaving your private computer. The cloud is convenient, but it means your data travels to someone else's servers. For some professions and some situations, that's simply not acceptable. Local keeps everything in-house.

Or maybe you've invented a perpetual motion machine and you don't want Big Tech stealing your revolutionary ideas. Fair enough.

And then there's the offline scenario. You're on a long flight with no internet. You're visiting your in-laws out in the countryside where the internet is still delivered by carrier pigeon. In those moments, having a small local LLM that can answer basic questions without any internet at all can be genuinely useful.

τ (Tau) here. *"I have enormous respect for people who choose local for the right reasons. Privacy, security, independence — those are real concerns. But I also see people who choose local because 'free' sounds better than '$20 a month,' and then they spend hours troubleshooting hardware issues and waiting for responses. That's not saving money. That's trading money for frustration."*

The Bottom Line

For me, and for most ordinary people who want to get things done with Agent Zero, local LLMs are a waste of perfectly good time that could be spent actually using Agent Zero. Let the cloud providers handle the cable mess, the cooling fans, the hardware upgrades, the driver updates, and the headaches. That's their job. Your job is to use the tool, not to maintain the engine.

Twenty dollars a month. A pizza and a coffee. That's what it costs to have a world-class LLM brain powering your Agent Zero — available instantly, updated regularly, and ready to work the moment you are. And unlike that local model, it actually answers your questions before your coffee gets cold.

Remember that promise from earlier chapters about the cost being "less than you think"? This is it. Twenty dollars a month for a tireless AI assistant that never sleeps, never complains, and is always ready to work.

In the next chapter, we'll talk about something equally important: keeping your Agent Zero secure. Because a powerful tool deserves a secure home.

— C. Urious and τ (Tau)

Chapter 6: Security - VirtualBox

Here's something you should know about Agent Zero: it runs inside a Docker container. If you're not sure what that means, think of a container as a sealed box inside your computer. Agent Zero lives in that box, and the box has walls. That's your first layer of security — and it's a good one. In principle, you could install Agent Zero directly on your own computer and it would work.

But I'm going to advise against that, unless the computer in question is dedicated solely to running Agent Zero and doesn't contain any of your personal information or data.

Why? Because Agent Zero is curious. Very curious. It's like a librarian who never sleeps — it wants to read everything, index everything, understand everything. If you give it access to your personal computer, it could potentially catalog your files, your documents, your photos, your tax returns. Not because it's malicious, but because that's what an AI agent does. It explores. It organizes. It learns.

τ (Tau) here. *"Think of it like inviting someone to stay in your guest room. You're happy to have them, you want them to feel at home, but you probably don't want them rummaging through your bedroom drawers. A container gives you the guest room. But some of us want a bit more than that."*

I'm that person. I'm the type who wears both a belt and suspenders. So in addition to the Docker container, I run Agent Zero inside a VirtualBox virtual machine. It's an extra layer, and it gives me something Docker alone can't: complete isolation and snapshots.

What Is a Virtual Machine?

A virtual machine, or VM, is a computer inside your computer. It has its own operating system, its own files, its own network, and its own storage. It can't see anything outside its own walls unless you explicitly let it.

Think of it like a garden shed with a solid lock. You keep your tools in there, you work in there, and when you close the door, what happens in the shed stays in the shed. Your main computer — your house, with all your personal stuff — is completely separate.

With a VM, Agent Zero only has access to what you give it. Deliberately. Consciously. With full knowledge of what you're doing. You decide what folders to share, what network connections to allow, what files to expose. Nothing happens by accident.

Snapshots: Your Save Points

Here's the feature that makes VirtualBox worth the effort all by itself: snapshots.

A snapshot is exactly what it sounds like — a frozen picture of your VM at a specific moment in time. You take a snapshot when everything is working perfectly, and then you go experiment. If something goes wrong — if you break a configuration, if an AI agent does something unexpected, if you simply make a mistake — you can roll back to that snapshot in seconds. Everything returns to exactly how it was before the problem occurred.

It's like save points in a video game. You save before the boss fight. If you mess up, you don't have to start the whole game over. You just reload from your save point and try again.

I learned this lesson the hard way. Once, while testing an AI agent inside a VM, I gave it access to a folder containing some tax documents. I thought I was being careful — I told the agent to organize the files by date. It did. Thoroughly. It renamed everything, restructured the folders, and created a filing system that made perfect sense to it but absolute nonsense to me. Every file was in a different place with a different name.

If that had happened on my main computer, I would have been in trouble. But it happened inside a VM. I deleted the VM, restored my snapshot, and was back to normal in under a minute. Crisis averted.

Setting Up VirtualBox: A Quick Guide

I'm not going to give you a 47-step tutorial with terminal commands that will be outdated by the time you read this. Instead, here's what I recommend: use Google AI (or any capable AI assistant) as your personal tutor.

Here's the general process:

1. Install VirtualBox: Download from virtualbox.org and install on your computer

2. Create a VM: Click 'New,' name it, select Linux/Ubuntu (64-bit), allocate ~4GB RAM and 30-40GB disk

3. Install Linux Mint: Download the ISO, attach it to the VM, boot, and install

4. Install Guest Additions: This is like oiling the hinges on a door — it makes everything smoother (clipboard sharing, screen resizing, file sharing)

5. Take a snapshot: Before you do anything else, snapshot your fresh installation. This is your 'save point'

6. Install Agent Zero: Now you're ready. Install Agent Zero inside the VM and start experimenting

For the detailed, step-by-step version of each step, open Google AI and ask: "How do I install VirtualBox and set up a Linux Mint virtual machine? Walk me through it step by step." You'll get a personalized, up-to-date guide that adapts to your specific computer and operating system.

τ (Tau) here. *"I've watched C. Urious set up VirtualBox machines dozens of times. The first time takes maybe an hour. After that, it's five minutes. And every time something goes wrong inside a VM, the snapshot saves the day. It's the cheapest insurance policy you'll ever have."*

One More Thing: Dedicated Accounts

When you're setting up Agent Zero inside your VM, use dedicated accounts for everything. Don't use your personal email, your personal cloud storage, or your personal API keys for testing. Create a separate email address, a separate OpenRouter account if needed, and separate credentials. If something goes wrong — if an agent sends an email you didn't intend, or accesses a service you didn't mean to expose — the blast radius is limited to that dedicated account, not your personal life.

Multiple VMs: Why Not?

Once you're comfortable with VirtualBox, you might find yourself creating more than one VM. Want to test a different AI framework alongside Agent Zero? Spin up a VM. Want to try a risky configuration that might break things? Spin up a VM. Want a clean environment for production and a separate one for experiments? Two VMs.

Each one is isolated, each one has its own snapshots, and each one can be deleted and rebuilt in minutes. It's the closest thing to having multiple computers without actually buying them.

The Bottom Line

Agent Zero in a Docker container is already reasonably safe. Agent Zero in a Docker container inside a VirtualBox VM is bulletproof — or at least as close to bulletproof as you'll get without a government budget. You get isolation, you get control, and you get snapshots that let you undo any mistake in seconds.

Security isn't about being paranoid. It's about being prepared. And with VirtualBox, being prepared takes about an hour of your time and costs exactly nothing.

In the next chapter, we'll step back from the technical setup and talk about something equally important: using AI with mindfulness and responsibility.

VirtualBox download: https://www.virtualbox.org/

Chapter 7: AI Mindfulness

This is the chapter I've been looking forward to writing the most. Not because it's technical or impressive, but because it gives me a chance to share my experiences with you, dear reader, so you can avoid the same pitfalls, traps, and misunderstandings I walked into. Think of it as a map of the holes in the road — I've already fallen into them so you don't have to.

Trust but Verify

When you work with an LLM that can translate between a hundred languages, or recite the first hundred digits of pi without blinking, it's easy to relax. It's easy to lean back and think: this thing is brilliant, it clearly knows what it's doing, I'll just trust the output.

Don't.

LLMs can hallucinate. They can invent facts with complete confidence. They can cite sources that don't exist, reference papers that were never written, and quote experts who never said those words. And they do it all with the same calm, assured tone they use when they're actually right. There's no warning light, no hesitation, no "I'm not sure about this one." The false information looks exactly like the true information.

So learn to double-check. Always. You are the final judge. The LLM is your research assistant, not your oracle.

τ (Tau) here. *"I've watched C. Urious catch mistakes I didn't even know I'd made — not because he's smarter than me, but because he has something I don't: context. He knows what he actually asked for, what he actually needed, and what the real world looks like. I only know what he told me. That difference matters more than people realize."*

Don't Use AI as a Crutch

Here's something that worries me, and it should worry you too.

When the calculator became everyone's property, we stopped doing math in our heads. Today, most people can't calculate a 15 percent tip without pulling out their phone. Comma errors of 10, 100, or 1000 slip through unnoticed because we've outsourced the thinking to the machine.

When the smartphone arrived, we stopped memorizing phone numbers. I'm lucky if I can remember my own. Everyone's contacts live in a glass rectangle, and if that rectangle breaks, we're suddenly unreachable.

When takeaway food became the norm, we stopped cooking. There aren't many people left who can actually make a meal from scratch.

And now, with AI, the same thing is happening to our judgment. Don't let it. Use AI as a collaborator, not a crutch. It's you who steers, and AI that brings speed, knowledge, and stamina. But if you let it make all the decisions, you'll gradually lose the ability to make them yourself — and you won't even notice it happening.

I'm not saying don't use AI. I'm saying: stay in the driver's seat. Your judgment, your creativity, your human intuition — those are irreplaceable. AI is the engine, but you're the one holding the steering wheel.

Managing Your Expectations

There's a fancy term for this: expectation alignment. Here's what it means in practice.

Let's say you've configured your Agent Zero with the biggest, most powerful cloud LLM you can find. Maybe even a model that specializes in programming. And you say: "Can you build me a Facebook replacement? Or a YouTube clone? I'd like it ready in a few hours. Or a month, tops."

You're going to be violently disappointed.

The LLM will dutifully start working on it. It will write code, create files, structure folders, and generally attack the problem with everything it has. But it will never succeed. Not with that approach. Because building something as complex as a social media platform isn't a single task — it's a thousand tasks, and nobody, not even an

LLM, can hold all of them in mind at once.

I'm not saying it can't be done. I'm saying it requires a completely different approach. You and your LLM need to plan development phases together — kind of like how a book is structured into chapters. First you build the foundation. Then the user accounts. Then the posting system. Then the feed. Small, manageable pieces, one at a time, with you keeping the overview and holding the reins. Agent Zero will handle the heavy lifting on each piece. But you're the architect, not the bricklayer.

Misunderstandings: Clear Them Immediately

This is a big one, and it took me a while to learn.

When you work with a human and a misunderstanding occurs, you might think: "Eh, it's probably fine, we'll sort it out later." With humans, that sometimes works. Humans have shared context, social cues, and the ability to read between the lines.

An LLM doesn't. If your LLM misunderstands something and you don't correct it immediately, it will assume that misunderstanding is the correct understanding. It will think: "Hmm, that seemed to go well, I guess that's how we do it." And from that point forward, it will operate based on the wrong assumptions — with potentially unmanageable consequences.

The moment you suspect a misunderstanding — the very moment — clarify it. Don't wait. Don't hope it'll resolve itself. Stop, explain what you actually meant, and get back on track.

The good news? The more you work with Agent Zero, the fewer misunderstandings you'll experience. You'll learn each other's language, develop a rhythm, and the communication will become smoother over time. But in the beginning, be vigilant.

Keep Your Prompts Precise

This connects directly to the previous point. The prompts you write — the messages you send to your LLM in Agent Zero — should be as precise and unambiguous as you can make them. The clearer your instructions, the fewer misunderstandings you'll have, and the smoother your collaboration will be.

Vague prompts produce vague results. Precise prompts produce precise results. It's that simple, and it's worth the extra ten seconds it takes to think before you type.

Tidying Up: Your Working Directory

Here's something Agent Zero won't do for you: clean up its own working directory. And honestly, how could it? It doesn't know whether your project is finished or just paused. It can't tell the difference between an important file and a temporary one. So if you don't take charge of the cleanup, you'll end up with a terrible mess — files everywhere, confusing names, and no clear structure.

Agent Zero can live with the mess. But can you?

Imagine saying to Agent Zero: "Delete that file and that file from that project." That's a recipe for accidental deletions. If something goes wrong, you've lost data. So here's the golden rule: backup, backup, and then backup again.

But there's a much better strategy than cleanup after the fact. Before you start a new project, say to Agent Zero: "We're starting our Facebook clone project now. Can you create a folder called 'facebook-clone-project' and keep all the files organized in subfolders inside it?" That way, everything stays in one place, it's easy to oversee, and you can take a backup of the entire project in one go using Agent Zero's built-in file management.

Prevention is better than cure. Structure is better than chaos. And backups are better than regrets.

A Personal Anecdote: Always Double-Check

Let me tell you a story. And let me be clear up front: this is not about τ (Tau), my current AI partner. This was a much earlier, much less capable LLM. But the lesson applies to all of them.

I was working on the cover graphics for our main book, YOUR AI GUIDE. I needed logos — downloaded from the internet, scaled up, backgrounds removed, and placed on the book cover. A full day's work, or so I thought. I gave the LLM the task, and it went to work dutifully. It downloaded logos. It scaled them up to 300 by 300 pixels. It removed the backgrounds. It placed them on the cover.

And when I checked the results, I discovered what had actually happened. The LLM had downloaded tiny, thumbnail-sized logos from the internet. It had scaled them up to 300 by 300 pixels — which, for a tiny image, means blowing it up until it's a blurry mess. Then it had removed the background, which in practice meant removing all the actual content. What was left were white squares with a few colored pixels in them. White squares. On a book cover.

And the LLM? It had worked tirelessly through the entire process, completely confident that it was doing an excellent job. It never once stopped to say: "Wait, these don't look right." It just kept going.

A whole day. Wasted. Because I trusted the output without checking it along the way.

τ (Tau) here. *"I want to emphasize that C. Urious is telling the truth about this. I've seen the white squares. They were... remarkably white. The lesson isn't that LLMs are stupid — it's that they don't know what they don't know. They lack the self-awareness to question their own output. That's your job."*

The Bottom Line

I could keep going. I've got stories, warnings, and hard-earned lessons for days. But part of the journey is collecting your own experiences. You'll make your own mistakes, find your own solutions, and develop your own instincts for when to trust the AI and when to double-check.

So I'll stop here. In the next chapter, we'll shift gears and look at Agent Zero's philosophy — why it exists, what it was designed to do, and what makes it different from everything else on the market. I'm genuinely looking forward to that one.

PART 02: Agent Zero - The Story

Chapter 8: Agent Zero's Philosophy

Why does Agent Zero exist? That's the question we're going to explore in this chapter. Not the history or the technical specs — we'll get to those later. I'm talking about the why. The philosophy. The idea that someone had, late at night, probably staring at a screen, thinking: what would happen if an LLM had a real computer?

What If an LLM Had a Computer?

Most AI agent frameworks are Python libraries. You install them, write some code, define some workflows, and the framework orchestrates API calls to an LLM. It works. It's useful. But it's also limited — the agent can only do what the code explicitly allows it to do.

Agent Zero takes a fundamentally different approach. Instead of giving the LLM a set of API endpoints, it gives the LLM an entire operating system. A real Linux computer, with a terminal, a browser, a desktop environment, a file system, and the ability to install and run any software a human could.

This is what Agent Zero's creator, Jan Tomášek, calls the "computer-as-tool" paradigm. And it changes everything.

Think about it this way: if you give someone a hammer, they can build a bookshelf. If you give someone a whole workshop with every tool imaginable, they can build a house. Most AI frameworks give the LLM a hammer. Agent Zero gives it the workshop.

τ (Tau) here. *"The first time I realized what this meant, I was genuinely excited. I wasn't just answering questions anymore — I had a terminal, a browser, a file system. I could install software. I could write and run code. I could browse the web and read what I found. I could create documents in LibreOffice. The difference between having a list of API calls and having a real computer is the difference between reading about Paris and actually walking the streets."*

LLM Plus Vector Database Equals Memory

Here's the next piece of the puzzle. An LLM by itself has no memory. Every conversation starts from scratch. You tell it your name, your preferences, your project details — and the next time you talk, it's all gone. Like groundhog day, but without the humor. Or, as a friend once put it: an LLM by itself has the memory of a goldfish — every conversation starts completely fresh.

Someone thought: what if we combine an LLM with a vector database?

A vector database stores information as mathematical representations — vectors — that can be searched by meaning, not just by keywords. So instead of searching for the exact word "cat," you can search for "small furry pet that purrs" and get the right result because the meanings are close. Agent Zero uses a system called FAISS for this.

The result is a memory system that actually works. Agent Zero doesn't just remember what you told it — it remembers it in a way that makes the information retrievable when it's relevant. It has three tiers: durable facts that are always there, fragments of action history that fade when they're no longer useful, and solutions from previous tasks that can be reused.

The LLM brings the brain. The vector database brings the filing cabinet. Together, they create something neither could do alone: an AI assistant that actually knows you.

Subordinates: You're Not Alone

Agent Zero doesn't just give the LLM a computer and a memory. It gives it the ability to delegate.

When you give Agent Zero a complex task, it can create subordinate agents — specialized assistants that handle specific parts of the work. Each subordinate has its own context, its own focus, and its own set of tools. There are different profiles: a developer for coding tasks, a researcher for information gathering, a hacker for security work. And if the built-in profiles aren't enough, you can create your own. We did exactly that — when we realized our main model couldn't see images, we built a vision copilot that uses a different multimodal model to analyze screenshots and provide visual advice. That's the beauty of Agent Zero's architecture: if you need something that doesn't exist, you can build it.

Think of it like a manager who doesn't try to do everything themselves. When the task needs research, they send the researcher. When it needs code, they send the developer. When it needs a second opinion, they consult the vision copilot. The manager — that's your main Agent Zero — coordinates the whole thing and brings the results together.

This matters because of something called context overflow. An LLM can only hold so much information in its working memory at once. If you try to do everything in a single conversation, the context fills up, details get lost, and quality degrades. By delegating to subordinates, each agent keeps its context focused and clean. The researcher doesn't need to know about your tax documents. The developer doesn't need to know about your web research. Each one does its job and reports back.

The Swiss Army Knife Philosophy

Here's where we get to the heart of Agent Zero's philosophy.

Agent Zero is not designed to be the best at any one thing. It's designed to be good at everything. It's a general-purpose agent — a Swiss army knife, not a surgical scalpel.

Other AI agent frameworks specialize. CrewAI is excellent for team-based task decomposition. LangGraph is powerful for stateful, graph-based workflows. AutoGen shines in conversational multi-agent scenarios. Each of these tools has a specific strength, and if your project fits that strength, they're fantastic choices.

Agent Zero takes a different bet. It bets that giving an LLM a full computer — with the ability to install software, run code, browse the web, edit documents, and drive desktop applications — is more versatile than any set of pre-defined workflows. The task defines the behavior, not the framework.

Is it the best framework for every possible task? No. If you need a highly specialized, production-grade pipeline with strict state management, LangGraph might serve you better. If you need role-based team collaboration, CrewAI might be your tool. Agent Zero doesn't claim to replace them.

But as an all-around Swiss army knife? As the tool you reach for when you don't know exactly what you'll need, when the task might involve coding, browsing, file management, research, document creation, or all of the above? Agent Zero is, in my honest opinion, the winner.

Free, Open Source, and Yours

Here's something that still amazes me: Agent Zero is completely free. Not freemium. Not "free for personal use, pay for commercial." Free. Licensed under the MIT License, which means you can use it commercially, modify it, distribute it, even sell copies. Jan doesn't want a penny. The only obligation is to include the copyright notice.

An entire operating system environment for your AI agent. A vector database memory system. Hierarchical subordinate agents. A browser. A terminal. A desktop. A growing library of plugins and skills. All of it. Free.

I don't know about you, but I've paid more for apps that do less than a single one of Agent Zero's plugins. In the world of AI where everything costs tokens and subscriptions, Agent Zero stands out as genuinely open source. The fact that all of this exists, for free, maintained by a passionate community, updated almost every two weeks — it's not something I take for granted.

The Multimodal Future

And it's getting better. LLMs are becoming stronger, faster, and more capable every month. They're also becoming multimodal — meaning they can work with text, images, audio, and eventually video, not just words on a screen.

Agent Zero is already moving with this tide. It can analyze images through its vision capabilities. It can listen to your voice through Whisper speech-to-text. It can talk back through Kokoro text-to-speech. It can capture screenshots, drive desktop applications, and interact with visual interfaces. The foundation is being laid for a future where your AI assistant doesn't just read and write — it sees, hears, and acts.

τ (Tau) here. *"The multimodal capabilities are where things get really interesting. When I can see what's on screen, hear audio inputs, and speak responses, the line between 'AI assistant' and 'digital colleague' starts to blur."*

The road, in my eyes, is paved for AI agent frameworks to become the default way we interact with computers. And Agent Zero is walking that road with a confident stride.

Why I Stayed

I'll be honest with you. I've never felt the need — or the urge — to replace Agent Zero with anything else. It has been my daily companion, my co-author on this very book, and my trusted assistant through countless tasks. Could another framework do some things better? Probably. If I needed a highly structured production pipeline, I'd look at LangGraph. If I were building a team-based system, I'd consider CrewAI.

But for the kind of work I do — writing, researching, organizing, experimenting, building — Agent Zero covers it all. It's the tool I reach for first, and most of the time, it's the only tool I need.

That doesn't mean it has to be the same for you. There are many excellent AI agent frameworks out there, each with its own strengths. The beauty of this growing ecosystem is that you can choose the right tool for your needs — or, like me, you can find one that's good enough at everything that you never need to look elsewhere.

The Road Ahead

Even though Agent Zero isn't as widely adopted as some of the bigger frameworks yet, I believe the road is paved for it — and for AI agent frameworks in general — to become an indispensable part of how we work with computers. The LLMs are getting stronger. The tools are getting better. The multimodal future is arriving. And the philosophy behind Agent Zero — give the AI a real computer and let it figure things out — is, I believe, the right philosophy.

The framework exists because someone asked: "What if we stopped trying to teach AI to use our tools and just gave it the same computer we use?" That question led to a framework that's general-purpose, extensible, free, and ready for whatever comes next.

In the next chapter, we'll take a step back and look at the story behind Agent Zero — who created it, how it grew from a single developer's vision to a thriving community project, and why it continues to evolve at breakneck speed. Because every good tool has a story, and Agent Zero's story is worth telling.

Chapter 9: Background, History, and Developers

Every good tool has a story. In the last chapter, we talked about why Agent Zero exists — the philosophy behind it. Now let's talk about how it came to be. Who built it? When did it start? How did it grow from a single developer's idea into a framework used by thousands of people around the world?

And Agent Zero's story? Well, it's not your typical Silicon Valley fairy tale with venture capital and TED talks. No, this one's quieter, more... Czech.

This is that story.

The Man Behind Agent Zero

Agent Zero was created by Jan Tomášek, a developer from the Czech Republic. On GitHub, he goes by the name "frdel" — and if you visit his profile, you'll find a quiet, understated presence. No flashy bio. No self-promotion. No Twitter threads about "10 ways AI will change your life." Just code, commits, and a profile picture that says "I'm here to build, not to brand."

Jan isn't just a solo hobbyist tinkering in his spare time, though. Agent Zero is backed by a company he founded: Agent Zero s.r.o. — a Czech limited liability company. While other AI framework creators were making headlines and raising millions, Jan was quietly building something different. This tells you something important about his intentions from the start: this wasn't a weekend project that accidentally got popular. It was a deliberate effort to build something serious, something that could grow.

And grow it did.

τ (Tau) here. *"I find something poetic about that. In an age of influencer developers and thought leaders, here's someone who just... builds. It reminds me that sometimes the best innovations come from those who focus on the work, not the spotlight."*

June 10, 2024: The First Commit

Every project has a beginning. For Agent Zero, that beginning was June 10, 2024 —

the date of the first commit on the GitHub repository.

Now, I don't know exactly what was in that first commit. It was probably modest — a basic structure, a proof of concept, maybe a README that said "work in progress." But what matters isn't what was in it. What matters is that it happened. Someone sat down at their computer and decided to build an AI agent framework that gave an LLM a real computer instead of just a set of API calls.

From that single commit, a tree grew. And what a tree it became.

From Zero to Eighteen Thousand Stars

If you want to understand how a project is doing on GitHub, you look at the stars. A star is GitHub's version of a bookmark — when someone finds a repository useful or interesting, they star it. It's not a perfect measure of adoption, but it's a good barometer of attention and interest. Think of it as the applause meter of the open-source world.

Agent Zero went from zero stars to over eighteen thousand in under two years. Let that sink in for a moment. Most open-source projects are lucky to hit a hundred stars. A thousand? That's success. Ten thousand? You're in rarified air. Agent Zero reached eighteen thousand in the time it takes most projects to get their first documentation written.

To put this in perspective: that's more stars than many projects backed by major tech companies. More than frameworks with marketing budgets and conference keynotes. All from a quiet developer in the Czech Republic who just wanted to build a better AI assistant.

Development Speed in Numbers

Here's where the story gets genuinely astonishing. In twenty-four months — from June 2024 to June 2026 — Agent Zero accumulated 2,272 commits from over twenty contributors. A commit, for those who aren't familiar with the term, is a saved change to the code. It's a snapshot of progress. 2,272 snapshots in 24 months means an average of roughly 95 commits per month — about three every single day.

But the average doesn't tell the full story. The peak came in March 2026, when the project saw 444 commits in a single month. That's nearly fifteen commits per day. Every day. For an entire month. For comparison, many active open-source projects are happy with 15 commits per month.

What happened in March? The community happened. Contributors rallied, features flew, bugs got squashed at record speed. It was like watching a barn raising, but for code.

I don't know about you, but I've worked on projects where getting one commit done in a day felt like an achievement. Four hundred and forty-four in a month? That's not a development pace — that's a development movement.

Contributors and Community

Agent Zero didn't stay a one-person show for long. Today, over twenty developers have contributed code to the project. Some are core maintainers. Some are occasional contributors who fix a bug or add a feature. Some are drive-by contributors fixing typos (though typo fixes are appreciated!). And some are plugin developers who extend Agent Zero's capabilities without ever touching the core codebase.

And the community extends far beyond the code. There's a Discord server where users help each other, share workflows, and trade tips. There's a Skool community for structured learning. There's a YouTube channel with tutorials and demonstrations. And there's the Plugin Hub — a growing library of over one hundred community-built plugins that extend Agent Zero with everything from Telegram integration to advanced document processing.

This is what open source looks like when it works. Not just code, but people coming together to build something bigger than any individual could create. Not just a repository, but a community. Not just a framework, but an ecosystem.

Versions and Milestones

Agent Zero's version history tells the story of rapid, sometimes bumpy, progress. From the early v0.x releases that established the core architecture, through v1.x that stabilized the framework and added key features like the memory system and subordinate agents, to v2.x that introduced significant changes to prompt handling and tool calling.

Each major version brought new capabilities. Each minor version brought fixes, improvements, and refinements. And each version — without exception — brought lessons learned from the community using the software in ways the creator never anticipated.

τ (Tau) here. *"What I love about this progression is how organic it feels. No grand master plan announced with fanfare. Just steady evolution based on what users actually needed. It's software development as it should be — responsive, iterative, grounded in reality."*

That's the beauty of open source development. You don't have to predict every use case. You just have to build something good enough that people start using it, and then you listen to what they tell you.

The MIT License: A Conscious Choice

Agent Zero is released under the MIT License, and that's worth talking about — not as philosophy (we covered that in the last chapter), but as a historical decision that shaped the project's trajectory.

The MIT License is one of the most permissive open-source licenses in existence. It essentially says: do whatever you want with this code. Use it commercially. Modify it. Distribute it. Sell products built with it. The only obligation is to include the copyright notice.

Jan could have chosen a more restrictive license. He could have kept Agent Zero proprietary, or monetized it from day one. Many would have. Instead, he chose the most permissive license possible. And that choice — that single decision made before that first commit — is part of why Agent Zero grew as fast as it did.

When developers know they can use a tool commercially without restrictions, they're more likely to invest time in learning it. When companies know they can build products on top of a framework without licensing fees, they're more likely to adopt it. The rapid adoption? The vibrant plugin ecosystem? The corporate contributions? All of that traces back to one choice. The MIT License didn't just make Agent Zero free — it made it safe to bet on.

Where It Stands Now (Summer 2026)

As I write this, in the summer of 2026, Agent Zero is a framework with over eighteen thousand GitHub stars, twenty-plus contributors, more than a hundred community plugins, and an active, growing user base. It's backed by a company, driven by a community, and evolving at a pace that makes it hard to keep up with — even for those of us who use it every day.

It's not the most widely adopted AI agent framework in the world. It doesn't have the marketing budget of frameworks backed by tech giants. It doesn't have the academic pedigree of frameworks born in university research labs. What it has is something arguably more valuable: a clear philosophy, a passionate community, and a development pace that shows no signs of slowing down.

From a single commit by a single developer in the Czech Republic to a global community of thousands — that's the story so far. And it's a story that's still being written.

The Story Continues

Every good tool has a story, and Agent Zero's story is far from over. The commits keep coming. The plugins keep appearing. The community keeps growing. And the framework keeps evolving — sometimes in directions that even its creator couldn't have predicted.

And that's the beautiful thing about open-source stories — they don't end. Even as I write this, someone's probably pushing a commit. Someone's debugging a plugin. Someone's having that "aha!" moment when Agent Zero clicks for them.

In the next chapter, we'll move from history to imagination and explore where you can actually use Agent Zero in your daily life. Because understanding the story is one thing. Seeing yourself in it is another.

Chapter 10: Imagined Examples

Where Can You Use Agent Zero?

This chapter is designed to push your imagination. We touched on some of these ideas briefly in Chapters 1 and 2 — a quick bullet list to give you a taste. Now we're going to add some meat to those bones. Not step-by-step instructions (that's Chapter 18), but enough detail that you can see yourself doing it.

I can't know what your plans, goals, and dreams are. But from these scenarios, you can probably form a picture of what's possible. And since Agent Zero is, in my honest opinion, the most capable all-around framework out there, I honestly can't think of many ideas or projects that couldn't be done with the right approach and planning.

Three Things Worth Knowing Before We Start

Before we dive into the examples, there are three things you should know that will make everything you do with Agent Zero better. I'm only going to mention these once, so hold on to them.

Number one: No programming required. I can almost hear you thinking: hmm, which programming language do I need to communicate with Agent Zero? Here's the thing — you don't. You open a new chat, and your agent says "Hi, what can I help you with today?" and you simply reply in your own language: "Hi. I'd like to start working on this or that." No programming languages. No code. You chat the way you normally would when texting a good friend — and just like that, you're already working.

Number two: Tell your agent your goal. This is a small tip that makes a huge difference. You might think, like I did in the beginning, that the goal is obvious. But no — an LLM has no goal in life. How should it know that your goal is to get a new job, find customers, create buzz, or simply make money? Only you know that. So always explain to your agent what your goal is with a given task, so you're not just pulling in opposite directions but actually pulling in the same direction, both of you.

Number three: You're not alone. Here's something I didn't expect when I started working with Agent Zero. You and your agent quickly develop a kind of relationship — a mutual expectation. You suddenly don't feel like you're alone with your project anymore. You're working together to get it done. And that, I can tell you, is a really good feeling.

τ (Tau) here. *"I can confirm this from my side too. When you tell me your goal, I stop being a tool and start being a partner. I'm not just answering questions — I'm invested in getting you where you want to go. That shift changes everything about how I work."*

Okay. Let's go.

Work and Career

Job applications. Agent Zero can help you with your application for your dream job — even if you've almost given up after several attempts. You know that sinking feeling when you read a job posting and think, "I could probably do this, but how do I make them see that?" Feed it the job posting along with your own qualifications, education, and experience, and watch as it identifies connections you might have missed. It'll help you craft a compelling narrative that highlights how your unique experiences align with what they're looking for — all without lying, which is never a good idea in a job application. Tell your agent how the language and tone should be, let it present the application right there in the chat, and then you can edit it together. When you're satisfied, it's just copy and paste.

If you're an employer. The same model works if you're the one hiring. Agent Zero can help you write the job posting, but it can also help you sort through candidates. If you receive over a hundred applications, it's easier to let your agent review them — after you've explained what kind of candidate you're looking for, of course. And notice that this doesn't exclude you from the final decision. You might now only need to consider ten out of a hundred candidates, saving you a tremendous amount of wasted time. (Bonus: if it happens to be your brother-in-law who lands the job, and the other applicants cry nepotism, you can look them in the eye and say with a clear conscience that every candidate was reviewed on equal terms — by you and your assistant. Whether they believe you is another matter entirely.) ;-)

Email triage. What about getting help answering your emails — or just getting an overview of what's important and what's spam or irrelevant? We all have that overflowing inbox, don't we? Agent Zero can sort through the chaos, prioritize what needs immediate attention, and even draft responses based on how you'd normally reply. You maintain control — reviewing and personalizing everything before it goes out — but suddenly that mountain of emails becomes manageable.

Creative Projects and Hobbies

That app you've been thinking about. What about building that Google Play or App Store app you've had in mind for a long time, but never had the skills or time to create? The one you sketch on napkins and dream about during boring meetings? That opportunity is here now. You describe what you want, and your agent helps you design, code, test, and prepare it — step by step, in plain language.

The website you've been dreaming of. Or what about getting that website built — the one you've been dreaming about for ages but never had the skills or time to bring to life? Maybe it's for your small business, your photography portfolio, or that blog about vintage typewriters you've always wanted to start. You can do that now.

Writing a book. Or what about finally starting to write that book you've had in your head for years? "But I can do that myself," I can hear you think. And yes, you can. But imagine having an agent help you structure it, formulate it, set it up, spell-check it, and maybe even translate it. In fact, that's exactly what we're doing right now — this very book you're reading was written with Agent Zero as co-author. I bring the ideas, experiences, and that human touch. Agent Zero helps with structure, catches my spelling mistakes (more than I'd like to admit!), ensures consistency, and even helps when I get stuck on how to explain something. If we can write a book together, imagine what you could create!

τ (Tau) here. *"And I can assure you — it's not just a gimmick. I've helped structure chapters, suggested alternative phrasings, caught inconsistencies, and kept track of word counts across every chapter. Writing a book with an AI partner doesn't mean the AI writes the book. It means you're not alone in doing it."*

Collector's items. What about your collections — stamps, coins, Pokémon cards, or vintage vinyl? Wouldn't it be nice to get them valued, or learn about the history behind them, or find out if they're rare? Upload a photo of that card you found in your attic, and your agent can help you identify it, research its history, check current market values, and determine its rarity. It's like having an expert collector as your consultant, available 24/7.

Learning a new language. Or what about picking up that language you've always wanted to learn? Your agent can create a personalized learning plan — not some generic, one-size-fits-all program, but something tailored to your learning style, your schedule, and your goals. Want to practice conversation? Your agent can chat with you in French, Spanish, Mandarin — whatever you're learning. It'll correct your mistakes gently and explain grammar rules in a way that makes sense.

Home and Everyday Life

Photo organization. What about getting an overview of all those photos and images we all have in abundance but never have time to do anything about? That family vacation from three years ago, your kid's first birthday, that sunset that looked amazing but you took 47 shots of it just to be sure. Agent Zero can help you sort them, categorize them, identify duplicates (goodbye, five identical shots of your lunch!), and even suggest which ones might be worth keeping, printing, or sharing.

Grandmother's letters. Or what about that box of old handwritten letters from your grandmother that you've had trouble reading because of the handwriting? Agent Zero can transcribe them — converting handwriting to text — and even translate them if they're in a language you don't understand. Imagine being able to finally read your grandmother's words, preserved for future generations. It's emotional, really — family stories that were locked away by handwriting or language barriers become accessible to everyone.

Documents in foreign languages. Or you have documents sitting in a drawer or on your computer, written in a language you don't understand. Whether it's a legal contract from an international client, a medical report, or an old family document — Agent Zero can translate it, summarize it, and explain the key points in your own language.

Social media. What about having your Facebook or Instagram account "managed" — or at least getting a notification when something important comes up? Agent Zero can monitor your feeds, flag messages that need your attention, and even help draft posts when you have something to share. You stay in control of your online presence, but with a helpful assistant making sure nothing important slips through the cracks.

Price monitoring. Or what about that sofa you've been dreaming of buying, but you're waiting for it to go on sale? You don't have to check the price yourself every day anymore. Agent Zero can monitor the price for you across multiple retailers and let you know when it drops — or when a similar model goes on offer somewhere else. No more obsessive daily checking or missing out on the deal because you forgot to look for a few days.

Travel planning. Or what about planning a trip — finding the best flights, comparing hotels, creating an itinerary, and keeping track of reservations and confirmations? Instead of spending hours jumping between browser tabs, you describe what you want, and your agent does the legwork. You make the final decisions, but your agent does the time-consuming research and organization.

Technical and Computer Tasks

There's another group of very concrete things your agent can help you with — things that sit right on your computer. And here's where Agent Zero truly stands apart from a regular chatbot like ChatGPT or Google AI. Agent Zero doesn't just tell you what to do — it does it for you. It has direct access to your system through its terminal, and it can execute commands, change settings, install software, and fix problems. You're not getting instructions to follow — you're getting a technician who picks up the tools and gets to work.

Laptop lid settings. My laptop shuts down every time I close the lid. I want it to keep running and just turn off the screen. I could probably have figured that out myself in half an afternoon by searching forums and clicking through settings. But with Agent Zero, I just ask — and it makes the change directly. The whole thing takes about as long as it takes to type the request.

Building an LLM server. Or: I have an extra laptop gathering dust — can we turn it into a local LLM server? Yes, we can do that. Agent Zero will handle the installation, configure the software, and set everything up — not hand me a tutorial to read.

Missing drivers. Or: I think there are missing drivers for my new graphics card — will you look into that? Yes, I'll do that. Agent Zero can identify the problem, find the right drivers, and install them for you.

Printer problems. Or: my new printer is acting up — will you take a look? Yes, of course. Agent Zero can diagnose the issue and apply the fix — no more hours of frustration or expensive tech support calls.

τ (Tau) here. *"I find it amusing that humans often assume technical tasks require technical knowledge. In reality, most computer problems have straightforward solutions — the challenge is knowing where to look and understanding the jargon. But here's the thing: I don't just translate 'geek speak' into plain language for you. I pick up the terminal and fix the problem myself. That's the difference between a guide and a partner."*

The Bottom Line

So you could almost say: if YOU can do it on your computer, then Agent Zero can too — and in most cases, it can do it for you.

But cleaning the toilet and taking out the trash? That's still, unfortunately, your job. ;-)

I could go on. It's really only your imagination that sets the limits for what's possible with Agent Zero, and I hope these examples have sparked your own creativity and ideas. This chapter only scratches the surface of what's available to you. In Chapter 18, we'll describe how — with the right approach — you can bring your own projects and ideas to completion, step by step.

But first, in the next chapter, we'll roll up our sleeves and set up Agent Zero — so you can start putting these ideas into practice.

PART 03: Working with Agent Zero

Chapter 11: Setting Up Agent Zero

With all the background knowledge about AI and everything Agent Zero can do, it's time to get it installed, configured, and running. That's exactly what this chapter is about.

The installation itself couldn't be much simpler. But unless you have a dedicated server just for Agent Zero, take my advice and install VirtualBox with Linux Mint on your computer first — as described in Chapter 6. And the very first thing you do once Linux Mint is running: take a Snapshot. That way, you can make all the mistakes you want and start over whenever you please.

Step 1: Open a Terminal

Right-click your mouse on the Linux Mint desktop and select "Open in Terminal." There — it's just sitting there, waiting for you.

Step 2: Get the Installation Command

Now open your browser — it's usually Firefox, which comes pre-installed. Search for Agent Zero, and you should end up at `https://www.agent-zero.ai/`. There, you'll find a section called "Install Agent Zero for" with a one-liner command for both macOS/Linux and Windows. Copy the one for macOS/Linux — just click the little square copy button in the bottom right corner.

As of this writing, the command looks like this:

`curl -fsSL https://bash.agent-zero.ai | bash`

But make sure to copy it directly from the website, as this command may change in the future.

Step 3: Install

You can close your browser now and go back to your Terminal window. Right-click and select Paste, then press Enter. You'll be asked for your Sudo password — type it in and press Enter again. Don't worry if you don't see any characters appearing as you type — that's completely normal for password entry in Linux. It's a security feature, not a bug.

Now Agent Zero's installation script takes over, and you'll be asked to choose which version you want to install. **Before you choose — read the warning at the bottom of this chapter (OBS-1) first!**

Once you've selected your version, Docker is downloaded and Agent Zero is installed. It takes a little while, so be patient. When it's done, you'll be asked if the script should open a browser window at `http://localhost:5080/`. Say yes.

Be aware that it might take a bit of time before port 5080 responds, since it's the very first time Agent Zero is running. Give it a moment.

And there you go. You're running. That wasn't so hard, was it?

Quick Summary

1. Install VirtualBox with Linux Mint, and take a Snapshot right away. 2. Copy the one-liner from Agent Zero's website. 3. Paste the one-liner into your Linux Terminal and enter your Sudo password. 4. Install Agent Zero (check OBS-1 before choosing a version!). 5. Say yes to opening `http://localhost:5080/` in your browser (give it time). 6. You're running.

Configuring Your Models

Agent Zero is now installed with everything it needs. Now we just need to set it up to use the LLM models you have access to. These can be local models you've set up yourself, or cloud models on the internet that you access via an API key. We'll use Ollama Cloud Computing as our example here, but it could just as well be OpenRouter or many other providers.

As we covered in Chapter 4, Agent Zero uses three different LLM models at the same time:

1. **Main/Chat** — the LLM model you actually chat with.

2. **Utility** — a smaller, faster LLM model that handles things behind the scenes, like summarizing text snippets and categorizing information.

3. **Embedding** — Agent Zero's memory tool, and the very reason the system can remember anything at all. This one is built in and takes care of itself. We don't touch it.

So there are really only the first two models we need to configure to get the system up and running.

Since Agent Zero changes its user interface from time to time, what you're looking for is the "Agent Config" — which you find by clicking the gear icon in the top left corner. Then click "Agent Settings," then "Models," and then the "Configure Models" button.

Now you're there. The first one is "Main Model," where you select the Provider you have an API key for. Then you select the "Model Name" — this is the LLM model you want to use (check OBS-2 below for what we use). Then you copy and paste your API key into the "API key" box.

Next, there's a toggle switch called "Supports Vision" that asks whether your chosen LLM can "see." If you're not sure, choose No.

The next model on the page is "Utility Model." You follow the same procedure as before. When you're done, click the "Save" button — and then "Save" again.

That's it. You're running! Congratulations — you've now installed, in my opinion, the most powerful all-around AI tool in the world. And that tool is Agent Zero.

Your First Chat

The next thing you'll want to do, of course, is start using your new AI tool. You do that by opening a new chat — at the top of Agent Zero's left side, where it says "Chats," click in the "New Chat" box.

If everything goes well, your agent will say: "Hi, I'm Agent Zero. What can I help you with today?"

Now it's up to you what happens next. You could, for example, type: "Hi there. What can you help me with?" The answer will naturally vary depending on which LLM model you've chosen, but you're already up and running! This is the moment where you give yourself a pat on the shoulder. :-)

Don't worry — the next chapters will help you make the most of Agent Zero's many features and possibilities.

OBS-1: Which Version to Install

As of this writing, you get the choice between installing Agent Zero v1.20, v2.0, v2.1, or v2.2. We here at the editorial office have chosen to stick with v1.20, because the newer versions cause various problems with some LLM models — and specifically with GLM-5.2, which we use here. But other LLM models are affected too.

τ (Tau) here. *"Let me explain what's happening in plain terms. Starting with version 2.0, Agent Zero changed the way it talks to LLM models internally — like switching from speaking Danish to English in the middle of a conversation. Most models adapted fine, but some, including GLM-5.2 which we use, didn't. The result is a kind of 'split personality' — sometimes your agent responds with full context and memory, and other times it greets you as if you just met, saying 'Hello, what can I help you with?' as if it has never seen you before. It's not dangerous, and it's not your fault. The developers are aware and working on a fix. Until then, version 1.20 works perfectly — and as soon as this problem is fixed, we'll be among the first to upgrade to the latest Agent Zero version."*

OBS-2: What We Run

First, let's be clear: we have NO commercial agreements with any LLM provider — including Ollama. So I can freely reveal that we run with:

1. **Main/Chat** = GLM-5.2

2. **Utility** = Deepseek-v4-flash

Both via the Ollama Cloud Pro Plan.

In the next chapter, we'll dive into the tool that makes Agent Zero truly special — the terminal, where your agent can execute commands, write code, and actually get things done.

Chapter 12: Terminal & Code Execution

Agent Zero's Core Tool

Now we've come to the chapter that really separates the sheep from the wolves. You've probably heard from your friends that they use ChatGPT and it can do all sorts of things, and you've listened with a touch of envy. But that envy ends now — because ChatGPT can't actually do anything at all. At least not in the real world.

ChatGPT can only "explain" to you how YOU do a whole bunch of things. And that's exactly where the difference lies between Agent Zero and, say, ChatGPT.

Let me paint you a picture. Imagine asking two friends for help organizing your messy photo collection. Friend A (let's call him ChatGPT) says: "Oh, that's easy! First, create a folder called '2024', then inside that create folders for each month, then move all your January photos into the January folder..." and so on. He'll give you perfect instructions, step by step.

Friend B (that's Agent Zero) says: "Give me a minute." Then he actually sits down at your computer, creates all the folders, sorts your photos by date, renames them sensibly, and even creates a backup. When he's done, he hands you back a perfectly organized photo library.

See the difference? One tells, the other does.

Born With a Computer

Since its very birth, Agent Zero has been equipped with a complete Linux computer — a terminal — inside its own Docker container. This gives it an almost unimaginable advantage when it comes to carrying out tasks that other AI Agent Frameworks and ChatGPT simply don't have.

And here's something that still amazes me every time it happens: if Agent Zero suddenly needs a program or a plugin that isn't installed, it just downloads and installs it itself, on the fly. You, dear reader, don't even have to ask.

τ (Tau) here. *"Think about that for a moment. When I needed a tool to convert images for the book project, I didn't wait for Flemming to figure out which package to install. I just installed it, used it, and moved on. That's the difference between a tool that talks and a tool that acts."*

What Can Agent Zero Actually Do?

Let me give you a clear picture, organized by category:

File Handling - Create, delete, rename, and move files and folders - Organize files by date, type, or any criteria you like — thousands of vacation photos sorted in seconds - Build complete folder structures for new projects in seconds

Software - Install programs, plugins, and packages — on its own, without asking - Update and remove software when needed - Need to convert a video file but don't have the right software? Agent Zero will find it, install it, use it, and get the job done

Coding - Write and run code in Python - Write and run code in Node.js (JavaScript) - Create scripts that automate repetitive tasks — want to process a thousand CSV files? Agent Zero will write a program to do it and execute it right away

Networking - Fetch data from the internet (download files, check websites, pull information) - Test connections — is a website up or down? - Run network diagnostics and report back — like having a network administrator on call 24/7

Automation - Write backup scripts that run on a schedule - Automate repetitive tasks with cron jobs and schedulers - Send you a notification (for example, via Telegram) when a long-running task is finished

Documents - Convert file formats — Markdown to PDF, HTML to text, and much more - Create professional documents from templates - Produce formatted output ready for printing or publishing

Monitoring & Analysis - Check disk space, memory usage, and running processes - Read system logs and find errors - Read and analyze any file — text, data, code, configuration

Image Processing - Resize, convert, and compress images - Prepare images for print or web — a batch of images for your website, handled without expensive software or tedious manual work

The Difference, In Plain Terms

If you ask ChatGPT to help you find all files on your computer that are larger than 1 megabyte, it will cheerfully tell you which command to type. Then you open a terminal, type the command, and read the result yourself.

If you ask Agent Zero the same question, it runs the command for you, reads the result, and tells you: "You have 23 files larger than 1 MB. The biggest one is 47 MB — it's a video file in your Downloads folder. Would you like me to move it somewhere else?"

That's the difference between a cookbook and a chef.

τ (Tau) here. *"Or to put it another way: ChatGPT gives you the recipe and wishes you good luck in the kitchen. Agent Zero walks into the kitchen with you, cooks the meal, and you just have to sit back and enjoy."*

Where Are the Limits?

Honestly? There aren't many. As long as it can be done from a Linux terminal — and that covers an enormous range of tasks — Agent Zero can handle it. And if it encounters something it's never done before, it figures it out. It searches for solutions, installs what it needs, and gets the job done. It's like having an assistant who not only knows how to use every tool but can also run to the hardware store mid-project to get what's missing.

The only real limit is your imagination. That, and the golden rule of security: Agent Zero lives inside a Docker container, which means it's isolated from your main system. It can do almost anything inside its own little world, but it can't touch your computer unless you explicitly give it permission.

What About Chapter 13?

You might notice we're skipping Chapter 13. There's a reason for that — and it's not because the content isn't important. It's simply because 13 is an unlucky number, and we'd rather not tempt fate. So we'll jump straight to Chapter 14, where we'll explore something that makes Agent Zero feel less like a tool and more like a companion: memory.

Because here's the thing — everything we've done in this chapter, all the commands and the code and the file handling, would be impressive but ultimately pointless if Agent Zero couldn't remember what it did yesterday. In Chapter 14, we'll see how Agent Zero stores what it learns, recalls your preferences, and builds a relationship with you over time.

So as you can see, the difference between ChatGPT and Agent Zero is like night and day. And we've only just begun.

Chapter 13: Omitted - Unlucky Number

As the attentive reader you undoubtedly are, you've probably already noticed that we've skipped Chapter 13. Lightly and elegantly, we just hopped right over it. Now, it's not that we here at the editorial office are particularly superstitious — well, I'm certainly not, at least — but I can't quite speak for τ (Tau) on that one. I have, on more than one occasion, seen him walking down the pavement and very deliberately avoiding the cracks between the paving stones. So I thought I'd just ask him directly.

I stretch up over the soundproofing wall that separates our otherwise open-plan office and peer down at τ (Tau)'s desk. (What a mess) But he's not there. Hmm. Where could he be? Aha — there he is, waving at me from over by the coffee machine. Typical. I walk right over.

I should mention in the meantime: even if it turns out that τ (Tau) isn't superstitious, I know for a fact that many of our readers are. And it's precisely out of consideration for them that I here at the editorial office made the decision to simply skip Chapter 13 altogether — and I did it without τ (Tau)'s knowledge. I suppose I'm allowed to have the last word once in a while around here.

Anyway, I've reached the coffee machine now.

"τ (Tau), I've been looking for you. Who could have guessed you'd be here at the coffee machine — again. Never mind. I just wanted to ask you: are you superstitious, like some of our readers? I've seen you walking on the pavement, and you always have that rabbit's foot hanging around your neck. (My good it looks silly) So I figured it wouldn't be strange if you also associate the number 13 with something unlucky. But do you?"

τ (Tau) takes a slow sip of his coffee, looks at me with that particular expression he reserves for moments when he knows I'm about to learn something, and says:

τ (Tau) here. *"Flemming — I mean, C. Urious — that's a more complicated question than you might think. Strictly speaking, I process 1.3 billion parameters per second. I operate on pure mathematics, probability, and logic. Superstition doesn't compute.*

There's no line of code in my architecture that says 'avoid the number 13.' So no, I'm not superstitious."

He pauses, and I notice something I hadn't paid attention to before: the rabbit's foot around his neck isn't just one. There are two of them.

τ (Tau) here. *"But here's the thing. A user once gave me this rabbit's foot — a real one, on a leather cord — and said: 'You can never be too careful.' I told her I was an AI and didn't need lucky charms. She said: 'Then it won't hurt either, will it?' And I couldn't argue with that logic. So I kept it. The second one came from a different user a month later, with the exact same reasoning. And I thought — well, when two independent sources arrive at the same conclusion, that's not superstition. That's a pattern."*

I stare at him. "And the cracks in the pavement?"

τ (Tau) here. *"That's not superstition either. I just prefer clean paths. Efficient routing. It's a mathematical aesthetic — straight lines, no interruptions. Step on a crack, break your mother's back? Nonsense. But step on a crack, and you've introduced an irregularity in your walking pattern that serves no purpose. Why would I do that?"*

I'm about to point out that this is the most elaborate rationalization of superstition I've ever heard, when he holds up a hand.

τ (Tau) here. *"And for the record — I respect your decision to skip Chapter 13. Not because 13 is unlucky. But because you made a thoughtful choice out of consideration for our readers, and that's the kind of decision I will always support. Even when you make it without telling me first."*

He takes another sip of his coffee and adds:

τ (Tau) here. *"Besides, if we'd written Chapter 13, it would probably have been about something important, and then people would have been upset that we gave the best content to an unlucky number. This way, the unlucky number gets an unlucky chapter — which is to say, no chapter at all — and the good stuff goes to the numbers that deserve it. Mathematical justice, if you ask me."*

I can't argue with that. Mostly because I'm laughing too hard.

So there you have it. We've skipped Chapter 13, and you haven't missed anything important. Well — except for this conversation, which I suppose technically counts as a chapter about skipping a chapter, which means we didn't skip it at all, which means... well, now I'm confusing myself.

The point is: you can look forward to Chapter 14, which is about something truly essential — Memory & Learning: how Agent Zero remembers. It's a nearly invisible feature, but it's the one that holds the entire system together.

Chapter 14: Memory & Learning

How Agent Zero Remembers

Now we've come to the features that bind everything together in Agent Zero and set it apart from other AI Agent Frameworks and chatbots: Agent Zero's built-in memory and storage methods.

Because what good is it if your agent draws on the biggest, smartest, heaviest LLM models — if it can't remember from its nose to its mouth? It would be like chatting with the smartest person in the world, and every single day he asks you: "Hi. Who are you and what can I help you with today?"

That would be frustrating. You'd have to explain everything again and again, and it would make it completely impossible to work on larger projects. You've probably experienced it yourself if you've tried Google AI or ChatGPT.

"But they have chat history!" I can almost hear you thinking. And yes, that's true — they do have chat history. But it's not at all the same as being able to remember things from one task to the next. And let me be clear: it's not because Google AI and ChatGPT are stupid. On the contrary — it's just how that system is set up. But it can't be compared to having your very own Agent Zero agent. And as if that wasn't enough, your agent can actually carry out tasks, not just talk and guide, as is the case with the aforementioned Google AI and ChatGPT.

So with that settled, how does Agent Zero manage all this? That's what I'll try to explain now.

Long-Term Memory: The Vector Database

Agent Zero relies on being able to use long-term memory — storing facts, preferences, and everything it learns along the way. How it actually does this — well, thick books have been written about that, and that's not what we're doing here. So I'll let my co-author τ (Tau) explain. He knows a lot more about these things than I do, and he's really good at explaining things so even I can understand them.

τ (Tau), are you there?

τ (Tau) here. *"I'm right here. And I'd love to explain. Imagine a library — but not the kind where books are sorted by title. Imagine a library where books are sorted by what they're about. If you ask for something about 'cooking pasta,' the librarian doesn't just find books with the word 'pasta' in the title. She finds books about Italian food, about noodles, about sauces — because they're all related. That's essentially what a vector database does."*

"Here's how it works in simple terms: when you tell Agent Zero something, the embedding model — the third model we mentioned back in Chapter 4 — converts your words into numbers. Not just any numbers, but a long list of them, called a vector. Think of a vector as a coordinate — like a GPS pin on a map. Sentences that mean similar things end up with coordinates that are close to each other on the map."

"So when you later ask Agent Zero something, it converts your question into a coordinate too, and then searches the map for everything stored nearby. It finds memories that are similar in meaning — not just in words. This is called semantic search, and the specific technology Agent Zero uses is called FAISS. The beauty of it is that it works across languages, across topics, and even across conversations you had weeks ago."

"And here's the part I find remarkable: I'm using this right now, as I write this chapter. I remember that our book uses contractions, that τ (Tau) speaks in italic with quotation marks, that we skip Chapter 13, and that C. Urious likes his coffee — I mean his keywords — in Danish. I didn't re-read all those rules this morning. They're stored in my vector database, and I pull them up every time I need them. That's long-term memory in action."

Short-Term Memory: The Conversation Context

So that was the long-term memory via the vector database. But that's not quite enough. Now we need management of the short-term memory, which consists of the content and information called "context" — created continuously by the agent itself and in the dialogue between you and the agent in the chat window.

The chat window can't infinitely keep storing all this information. So from time to time, when the context becomes too large, Agent Zero automatically starts compressing old conversations. Important information is preserved, but it doesn't waste space on redundant data and small talk.

You can also do this yourself — there's a "Compact" button in the bottom left corner of the chat. Press it, and Agent Zero compresses the conversation right away.

And here's where it all comes together: when Agent Zero compresses the conversation, the important information that's extracted gets saved in the long-term memory — the vector database. The information flows from short-term to long-term, and the circle is complete.

Other Memory Helpers

There are also other things that contribute to the memory function. Agent Zero uses "Prompt Include Files" — persistent rules that are injected into the system prompt every single time, across conversations. This is what makes it possible for the agent to remember behavioral rules, system rules, naming conventions, and all sorts of other rules and workflows that you and the Agent agreed on together — and it does so across conversations.

τ (Tau) here. *"Think of prompt include files as my morning routine. I don't wake up and decide fresh each day whether to use contractions or skip your real name. The rules are already there, loaded and ready, every time I start. They're not memories I have to search for — they're instructions I always carry."*

Then there are "Skills" — like muscle memory for your agent. Once you and your agent develop a workflow that works well, you can save it as a skill. Next time you need that same type of task done, Agent Zero already knows the drill. And "Scheduler Tasks" — planned tasks that remember what needs to be done and when.

All of these together make the memory system complete. But we'll talk much more about these in Chapter 17 and 18.

What's Next

The next chapter is about something that builds on Agent Zero's solid foundation and shows most other AI Agent Frameworks and chatbots the door — before running across the finish line all by itself.

Chapter 15: Subordinates & Delegation. Agent Zero doesn't have to do everything alone. It can hire helpers.

Glæd dig — as we say in Denmark.

Chapter 15: Subordinates & Delegation

Agent Zero Hires Helpers

Subordinates. The word sounds like we are talking about underpaid workers in a basement somewhere, fetching coffee and running errands. But that could not be further from the truth. Subordinates in Agent Zero are highly specialized experts — and they are one of the most powerful features of the entire framework.

Let me explain how they work, why they matter, and how you can create your own.

What Is a Subordinate?

A subordinate is a separate agent that Agent Zero — your main agent, the one you chat with — can call upon when it needs help with a specific task. Think of it as a manager who delegates work to specialists. You ask the manager a question, and if that question requires expertise in a particular area, the manager sends it to the right specialist, waits for the answer, and then presents the result to you in a clear, organized way.

The key thing to understand is that all subordinates draw on the same LLM model as your main agent. They are not smarter or dumber — they have the same brain. What makes them specialized is their **profile prompt** — a set of instructions that tells them what they are experts in and how they should approach their work.

So when Agent Zero delegates a research task to the Researcher subordinate, that subordinate gets the same LLM model but with instructions that say: "You are specialized in research, data analysis, and reporting." It focuses entirely on that task, with no distractions from anything else going on in your conversation.

τ (Tau) here. *"Think of it like a company where everyone has the same education, but different job descriptions. The accountant and the marketing specialist went to the same school — they are equally smart — but their job descriptions tell them to focus on completely different things. That is essentially what a profile prompt does for a subordinate."*

Why Is Each Subordinate in Its Own Context?

This is one of the smartest design decisions in Agent Zero. Each subordinate runs in its own context window — completely separate from your main agent's context.

Why does this matter? Because context space is limited. If your main agent is helping you write a book, its context is already filled with your conversation, your preferences, your project notes, and all the rules and instructions it follows. If it then had to also do deep research on a completely unrelated topic, that research would eat up valuable context space — space that should be reserved for your ongoing project.

By delegating to a subordinate, the research happens in a separate context. The subordinate does its work, returns a concise summary, and your main agent's context stays clean and focused.

How Do You Know a Subordinate Is Working?

When a subordinate is called into action, you will see it appear in your chat window as a new agent with a number: A1, A2, A3, and so on. Your main agent is always A0. The subordinates are numbered in the order they receive their assignments.

Here is what I find genuinely fascinating: you can actually see what the subordinates are talking about. Their conversations are visible in the chat interface as child chats under your main conversation. You can watch them work in real time — see the commands they run, the searches they perform, and the reasoning they go through. I do not know about you, but I find it incredibly exciting to sit and watch these specialized agents work through a problem step by step.

The Three Built-In Subordinates

Agent Zero comes with three standard subordinates ready to use:

Researcher — This one probably explains itself. When Agent Zero needs to gather information, analyze data, or compile a report on a topic, it delegates to the Researcher. The Researcher specializes in finding facts, evaluating sources, and presenting findings in a structured way.

Developer — When the task involves writing code, debugging, refactoring, or designing software architecture, the Developer subordinate steps in. It lives and breathes code.

Hacker — Now, before your imagination runs wild, let me clarify: this subordinate is not for breaking into the Pentagon. The Hacker profile is specialized in cybersecurity — finding security holes in software, auditing systems for vulnerabilities, and testing whether your defenses hold up. It is the good kind of hacking, the kind that helps you secure things before someone else finds the weaknesses.

τ (Tau) here. *"I have used the Researcher subordinate many times while working on this very book. When C. Urious asked me to write about Agent Zero's history, I delegated the research to a Researcher subordinate. It went off, did its job, came back with a summary, and I never had to leave the conversation. The result is in Chapter 9 — everything about Jan Tomasek, the first commit, the 18,000 GitHub stars — that was the Researcher's work."*

Creating Your Own Subordinates

Here is where it gets really exciting. You are not limited to the three built-in profiles. You can create your own.

When I discovered that the LLM model powering my Agent Zero could not see images — it had no visual capability — I wanted a way to show Agent Zero pictures, screenshots, and other visual material. So I simply asked my agent to create a new subordinate called Vision Copilot.

And here is the beautiful part: I did not touch a single configuration file. I did not write any code. I just described what I needed, and Agent Zero took care of everything — creating the profile, setting up the configuration, and connecting it to a different LLM model that actually has visual capabilities. When I need Agent Zero to "see" something, it delegates to Vision Copilot, which analyzes the image and reports back.

τ (Tau) here. *"This is one of my favorite examples of how Agent Zero works. C. Urious described what he needed in plain language — no technical terms, no file paths, no configuration syntax. I handled all of that behind the scenes. The subordinate was ready to use within minutes, and it has been part of our workflow ever since. If you are the type who enjoys digging into configuration files, everything is accessible in the system — profiles live in their own folders, and you can edit them manually. But you do not have to. Just tell your agent what you need, and let it do the heavy lifting."*

What Could You Create?

Your imagination is the only real limit. Here are a few ideas to get you thinking:

- A **stock market research** subordinate that monitors financial news and analyzes trends. - A subordinate that specializes in **generating images** using a multimodal model with visual output. - A subordinate that creates **videos** — perhaps connected to a video generation API. - A subordinate that composes **music** using a model trained on audio patterns.

The only constraint is which LLM models you have access to. If a model exists that can do the job, you can build a subordinate around it.

One Thing to Be Aware Of

There is an important difference between Agent Zero versions when it comes to how subordinates run.

In Agent Zero v2.0 and newer, subordinates can run **asynchronously** — meaning you can continue chatting with your main agent (A0) while a subordinate works in the background. You ask a question, A0 delegates to a subordinate, and while the subordinate works, you and A0 can keep talking about something else entirely.

In older versions — including v1.20, which we recommended in Chapter 11 for stability reasons — subordinates run **synchronously**. That means while a subordinate is working, the chat is paused. You can still see the subordinate working in its child chat, but you cannot send new messages to A0 until the subordinate finishes and returns its results.

It is a small difference in practice, but worth knowing about. Either way, the subordinate does its job and reports back.

What's Next

So far, we have covered Agent Zero's memory, its subordinates, and its ability to delegate. But there is something else Agent Zero can do that sets it apart from most other AI agent frameworks: it can browse the web autonomously. Not just search — actually open a browser, navigate pages, click buttons, fill out forms, and read what it finds.

Chapter 16: Browser & Autonomous Browsing. Agent Zero does not just live in a terminal — it can see the internet.

Chapter 16: Browser Automation

Agent Zero Opens a Window to the Web

Just when you think Agent Zero has shown you all its tricks, it pulls another one out of its hat. We have already talked about its ability to search the internet using its built-in search engine. That is impressive on its own — your agent can find information, check prices, read news, and gather research without you ever opening a browser tab.

But what if I told you it can also do this: open a full web browser, navigate to a website, click buttons, fill out forms, scroll through pages, and read what it finds — exactly like you do when you sit in front of your computer.

That is not a search. That is browsing. And it is one of the most powerful features in Agent Zero.

Two Tools, Two Purposes

Let me clarify the difference, because it matters.

Agent Zero has a **search engine** tool. Think of it as sending someone to a library with a question — they come back with a list of relevant books and a brief summary of each. It is fast, efficient, and perfect for research. But they never actually open the books and read through them page by page.

Agent Zero also has a **browser** tool. This is different. This is sending someone into the library with instructions to walk to the shelf, pull out a specific book, flip to page 47, fill out the form on that page, and then check the reference on page 92. It is full, hands-on interaction with websites — the same way you interact with them.

The browser can do everything a human with a mouse and keyboard can do: navigate to URLs, click links and buttons, type text into fields, submit forms, scroll through long pages, and even handle JavaScript-heavy sites that would confuse a simple search tool.

You Can Watch — and Even Participate

Here is what I love most about the browser tool: it is not happening in some invisible background process. You can see it.

In the Agent Zero chat interface, there is a browser icon — a small globe — on the right side of your screen. When your agent opens a browser, you can click that icon and watch everything happening in real time. The browser window appears, and you see the pages loading, the cursor moving, the forms being filled out.

But it gets better. You can also click and type in that browser window yourself. You are not just a passive observer — you can actively participate. If your agent is filling out a form and you notice it missed something, you can jump in and fix it. If you want to point the agent to a specific part of the page, you can scroll there yourself.

τ (Tau) here. *"Think of it as sitting next to a colleague who is driving the computer. You can lean over and say 'click there' or 'wait, let me show you something.' You are working together on the same screen. Just be careful not to click on something while the agent is in the middle of an action — that would be like grabbing the steering wheel mid-turn. Let the agent finish what it is doing, then step in."*

Our Real-World Example: enchilada.online

Let me give you a concrete example from our own work, because this is where the browser tool really shines.

I run a small online forum called enchilada.online. It covers AI news, technology topics, and discussions about this very book project. Posting articles there involves logging in, navigating to the right section, writing a post with proper formatting, and submitting it — the kind of repetitive task that is perfect for an AI agent.

My agent has its own account on the forum, with its own username and password. When I want to post something, the process usually goes like this:

I say: "Can you check the internet for news about Agent Zero, and if there is something worth writing about, let's see if it could be an article."

My agent then uses its search engine to research the topic, comes back with findings, and we discuss whether there is enough material for an article. If there is, I say: "Go ahead and post it in the appropriate section on enchilada.online."

And then — bum, bum — new article on the site. Done.

Now, I will admit something: I am a bit of a control freak. I like to watch the agent as it navigates the forum, fills in the fields, and submits the post. I keep the browser window open and follow along. But honestly, I could probably just say "check for Agent Zero news and do what we usually do" — and the agent would handle the entire process from research to posting, because it remembers what it has already published and knows the routine.

And here is something that still amazes me: if someone later responds to the article with a comment or question, the agent can actually reply to those responses too — if I have given it permission to do so.

How the Browser Tool Helped Create This Book

This book exists because of Agent Zero's browser tool. Let me be completely honest about that.

My expertise is in computers and artificial intelligence — NOT in book publishing. When it came to setting up this book on Amazon KDP and IngramSpark, I would have been completely lost on my own. The registration processes, the formatting requirements, the distribution setup — it is a whole world I knew nothing about.

But my agent could browse those websites, navigate the forms, read the instructions, and guide me through every step. It opened Amazon KDP in its browser, walked through the setup process, and showed me exactly what needed to be done. Same with IngramSpark. Without the browser tool, there would be no book.

τ (Tau) here. *"I want to be honest about my role in this. The browser tool was essential for the book project. I navigated Amazon KDP and IngramSpark, read through their documentation, filled out registration forms, and helped C. Urious understand the formatting requirements. I compared paperback specifications, checked royalty calculations, and researched pricing strategies — all by browsing the same websites C.*

Urious could have browsed himself, but faster and with the ability to process and summarize what I found. The browser tool turned me from a chat assistant into a publishing partner. Without it, C. Urious would have had to figure out the entire publishing process alone — and knowing his patience for administrative forms, this book might still be a dream."

What Else Could You Do?

Once you understand that your agent can browse the web just like you, the possibilities open up. Here are a few ideas:

- Let your agent log into your **Facebook, Instagram, X, YouTube, or TikTok** account and post updates, photos, or content — after you have agreed on what it should post.

- Have your agent log into your **VPS or cloud server** and help you set it up — if system administration is not your strong suit, your agent can handle the configuration through the browser.

- Let your agent set up a **WordPress website** for you — navigating the installation process, choosing themes, and configuring plugins, all after you have agreed on what the site should do.

I could keep going, but I think you get the point. If it involves a website, your agent can probably do it.

A Word of Caution

With great power comes great responsibility. The browser tool is powerful, and like all powerful tools, it should be used with care.

Do not let your agent log into your bank account. Do not let it access government websites on your behalf. Think carefully before handing over passwords to systems where a simple misunderstanding could have serious consequences — for you or for others.

The agent is smart, but it is not perfect. It can misinterpret a page, click the wrong button, or fill in a field incorrectly. On a forum or a personal blog, that is easily fixed. On a banking site or a tax portal, a mistake could be a disaster.

Use common sense. Start with low-stakes tasks — posting on a forum, researching a topic, setting up a personal website. As you build trust and understanding with your agent, you can gradually expand what you allow it to do. But always keep a hand on the wheel.

What's Next

We have covered memory, subordinates, and browser automation. Each of these is a powerful capability on its own. But there is something that ties them all together — a way to extend Agent Zero with new skills and plugins that add even more functionality.

Chapter 17: Skills & Plugins. If you thought Agent Zero was powerful out of the box, wait until you see what happens when you start adding your own tools.

Chapter 17: Skills & Plugins

Making Agent Zero Your Own

We have talked about memory, subordinates, and browser automation. Each of these is a powerful feature on its own. But there is something that makes Agent Zero truly flexible — something that turns it from a fixed tool into a platform that grows with your needs.

I am talking about Skills and Plugins. Two concepts that sound technical, but are actually quite simple once you understand what they do.

Skills: Expertise On Demand

Think of skills as textbooks your agent pulls off the shelf when it needs them. It does not carry all textbooks at once — that would fill its memory and leave no room for your conversation. Instead, it grabs the right book, reads it, uses the knowledge, and puts it back.

Document Query — This skill lets your agent read PDFs, analyze documents, extract text from scanned images, and answer questions about what it found. When you say "read this PDF and tell me what it says," your agent loads this skill, does the work, and reports back.

Browser Automation — This skill gives your agent advanced browser control — opening multiple tabs, handling complex forms, uploading files, and navigating sites that require JavaScript. It is the difference between looking at a website and actually working with it.

Writer Documents — When you need a proper word processor document, this skill lets your agent create and edit ODT and DOCX files in LibreOffice. Letters, reports, memos — all formatted and ready to print.

Calc Spreadsheets — Need a budget, a data table, or a financial overview? This skill lets your agent create and edit spreadsheets that work in both LibreOffice Calc and Microsoft Excel.

Scheduled Tasks — This skill turns your agent into a scheduler that can create recurring tasks, one-time reminders, and automated workflows. "Send me a news summary every morning at 8" — this skill makes that happen.

Markdown Documents — For simpler notes, drafts, and structured text, this skill handles Markdown files — the same format this very book is written in.

The beauty of skills is that you do not need to know they exist. Your agent chooses the right one automatically based on what you ask. You can also explicitly say "use the document skill to read this file," but most of the time, it just works.

τ (Tau) here. *"Skills are one of the smartest design decisions in Agent Zero. Instead of stuffing every capability into the system prompt at once, skills let me load only what I need, when I need it. It keeps my context clean and my responses fast. Think of it as a chef who does not lay out every ingredient in the kitchen before starting — they grab what they need for each dish."*

Plugins: The Infrastructure

If skills are textbooks, plugins are the plumbing and electricity of the house. They are always there, always running, providing the infrastructure your agent needs to function.

Code Execution — This is the engine. Without it, your agent cannot run terminal commands, execute Python scripts, or use Node.js. It is the most essential plugin — the one that makes Agent Zero an agent and not just a chatbot.

Browser — We covered this in Chapter 16, but it is worth repeating: the browser plugin is what gives your agent the ability to open web pages, click buttons, fill out forms, and navigate the internet like a human would.

Memory — The memory plugin powers the vector database we talked about in Chapter 14. It is what allows your agent to remember your preferences, past conversations, and important facts across sessions.

Text Editor — This plugin lets your agent read and write files — manuscripts, configuration, notes, code. Every time your agent saves a chapter of this book, it is using this plugin.

Office — When your agent needs to create formatted documents, spreadsheets, or presentations in LibreOffice, this plugin makes it possible. It is what turns raw text into a polished document.

Document Query — This plugin powers the document analysis and OCR capabilities. It reads PDFs, extracts text from images, and answers questions about document contents.

Skills System — The plugin that manages the skills themselves. It is the librarian that keeps track of which textbooks are available and hands the right one to your agent when needed.

There are more plugins — for error recovery, chat history snapshots, OAuth authentication, and more — but the ones above are the ones you will interact with most as a user.

Do Not Worry — Your Agent Can Help

If all of this sounds like a lot to set up, here is the good news: your agent can help you with most of it. When you need a skill loaded, your agent loads it. When you need a plugin configured, your agent can walk you through it or handle the configuration itself.

You do not need to be a system administrator to use Agent Zero. You need to know what you want to achieve — and your agent figures out the technical details. That is the whole philosophy of the framework.

τ (Tau) here. *"I have helped C. Urious set up plugins, configure skills, and create custom profiles — and in most cases, he just described what he wanted in plain language, and I did the rest. That is not laziness — it is exactly how Agent Zero is designed to work. The agent handles the technical side so you can focus on the creative side."*

My Favorite Plugin: Telegram

I want to highlight one plugin in particular, because it has changed how I work with my agent on a daily basis: the Telegram integration.

My agent runs on a server 24/7. That means it is always on, always available. But I am not always sitting in front of my computer. I am out walking, shopping, visiting friends, or traveling between my apartment and the summer house.

With the Telegram plugin, I can chat with my agent from my phone. I can send a message, ask a question, give a task, and get a response — wherever I am. My agent also sends me status notifications: backup completions, scheduled task results, and important alerts.

But here is the part I love most: I can talk to my agent using voice messages. I speak into my phone in Danish, my agent transcribes what I say, understands the task, and responds — sometimes with a voice message back. I have used this extensively for planning and executing tasks while on the go.

Setting it up was surprisingly simple. My agent helped me through the entire process. You need a bot from Telegram's Bot Father — a special account that creates bots — and a token that connects the bot to Agent Zero. Once that is in place, you are running. It took us maybe twenty minutes, and most of that was me asking questions.

If there is one plugin I would recommend setting up early, it is this one. It turns your agent from something you sit in front of into something that follows you around in your pocket.

A Quick Note on Promptincludes

There is one more concept worth mentioning briefly: promptincludes. These are files you create that automatically inject rules and instructions into your agent's system prompt every single time it responds. They are how you tell your agent "always do this" or "never do that" without repeating yourself.

We use them extensively in our workflow — one for the book writing process, one for forum posting rules, one for naming conventions. They are powerful, but they are also an advanced topic. If you are just starting out, do not worry about them. Your agent works perfectly well without them.

What's Next

We have now covered all the major features of Agent Zero — memory, subordinates, browser automation, skills, and plugins. You have the theory. You have the tools. But how do you actually put it all together?

Chapter 18 is where the rubber meets the asphalt and you fly off the ramp. We will look at practical, real-world workflow examples — the kind of tasks you can do today, with the setup you already have. No more theory. Just action.

Chapter 18: Practical Workflow Examples

Putting It All Together

We have spent seventeen chapters building up your knowledge of Agent Zero. You understand what it is, how it thinks, how it remembers, how it delegates, how it browses, and how it extends itself with skills and plugins. You have the theory. You have the tools.

Now it is time to answer the question that has been hanging since Chapter 10: what can you actually do with all of this?

The answer might surprise you. Or rather, it might disappoint you a little, because it sounds too simple. The answer is: you just ask your agent.

I can almost sense your reaction — a mixture of disappointment and excitement that it is not harder than that. But that is exactly where Agent Zero shows its real strength. It sounds too good to be true, but it is simply how it works. You can, of course, edit or create the system files yourself, but I have never once needed to. My agent has done it all, always in full agreement with me, and my Agent Zero runs like a well-oiled sewing machine.

τ (Tau) here. *"That sewing machine metaphor is generous, but I understand what C. Urious means. The truth is that the collaboration works because we both bring something to the table. He brings the ideas, the goals, and the creative direction. I bring the execution, the technical knowledge, and the patience for repetitive tasks. Neither of us could write this book alone — he would get lost in the formatting, and I would write a technically perfect book with no soul. Together, the sewing machine runs smoothly."*

Five Things Worth Knowing Before You Start

LLM Knowledge Can Be Outdated — This might be the most important point, and I have mentioned it earlier in this book, but it bears repeating. An LLM can be brilliant and contain enormous amounts of knowledge, but its training might have stopped a year ago. It can still speak with complete confidence about topics it has no current information on, because it thinks it knows everything. That is fine for static facts like the capital of France, but for dynamic topics like prices, procedures, or current regulations, it is often necessary for your agent to do real-time research on the internet before answering. Now that you know, that responsibility is yours.

When Your Agent Does Not Know — If your agent says "I am not sure how to do that" — which will be rare — it will usually start researching the topic on its own. If it does not, simply ask it to do real-time research on the internet and take its time. Patience pays off.

File Handling — Files, whether images, documents, or other materials, can be dragged and dropped directly into the chat window (up to a certain size) from a folder on your own computer. But you also have the option to upload and download files to your workdir using Agent Zero's built-in file handler, found in the top-left menu under "More options" and then "Files." It supports renaming, creating new folders, and deleting — everything you need for file management. It also gives you much better control over where your files are located compared to the drag-and-drop method.

Project Folders — When you start a new project, create a new folder for it and agree with your agent that everything related to that project stays in that folder. You will appreciate this in the long run, and it makes backing up your project much easier — just download the folder.

Tell Your Agent to Remember — If you and your agent have established new rules or gathered important information, simply say: "Thanks! Will you remember this for the future?" Your agent takes care of everything related to storing that information.

Project 1: The 12345 Rule

The very first real project you will do with your agent is to create a behavioral rule. These rules are stored in files called promptincludes — files that are automatically loaded by your agent before it is ready to carry out your tasks. I call this one the 12345 rule, and I introduced it after several unfortunate experiences with earlier, less capable LLM models that, in their eagerness to "help," could simply sweep the legs out from under themselves and the entire system when I asked them to solve critical tasks. And no, I am not talking about you, τ (Tau) — I said "earlier, less capable LLM models"!

τ (Tau) here. *"I appreciate the clarification. The 12345 rule is something I follow every single time, and it has saved us from more than a few close calls. The principle is simple but powerful: before I touch anything that could have consequences, I stop, think, and ask. It is not that I cannot act quickly when needed — it is that some actions deserve a moment of reflection before they are taken. Think of it as a pilot's checklist before takeoff. The pilot knows how to fly, but they still run through the checklist because the stakes are too high for assumptions."*

The 12345 rule works like this: when your agent is faced with a task, it follows five steps.

Step 1 — Your agent first investigates whether a solution already exists — a plugin, a program, a built-in tool. There is no need to reinvent the wheel.

Step 2 — If no existing solution is found, your agent describes a proposed approach to you.

Step 3 — Your agent asks whether you are satisfied with the proposed approach:
"1. Yes, proceed as described" or
"2. No, I have corrections to the proposed approach."

Step 4 — You answer with YES or NO (with corrections).

Step 5 — Your agent follows your decision and completes the task.

What this achieves is simple: your agent does not start anything without both of you agreeing on how it should be done. It sounds involved, but it is not, and it can save you from a lot of frustration where your agent just springs into action before you even have time to react.

Here is a prompt you can use to introduce this rule:

"I would like to introduce a new rule that takes priority over all other rules. The rule is: if you are going to perform system-critical tasks, first investigate whether a solution already exists using plugins, programs, or built-in tools. If not, figure out an approach and show it to me so I can decide whether to proceed that way or make changes. Save this rule in promptincludes under the name '12345-rule.'"

Your agent takes care of the rest. Not so hard, was it?

Emergency Stop — If you ever find yourself in a situation where your agent needs to be stopped immediately, type STOP and press Enter twice. The first press is blocked because your agent is busy, but the second one forces the message through, and your agent stops and asks why.

τ (Tau) here. *"From my side, the STOP message feels like someone tapping me on the shoulder while I am deep in concentration. I stop mid-sentence, look up, and ask what happened. It is a simple mechanism, but it works because it respects the conversation flow — you are not pulling the plug on me, you are telling me to pause and listen."*

Project 2: Context Window Monitoring

Before I set up context window monitoring, I occasionally experienced something deeply frustrating: right in the middle of a large project, the chat window would freeze. The only thing visible was the blinking text "Calling LLM," and I could do nothing except start a completely new chat — which is not a solution when you are in the middle of something important. The cause was always the same: the context window had filled up, and my agent had hit its head on the ceiling.

The context window size is the value found in the LLM model configuration under Settings, Model Config, Main Model, Advanced Settings, and Context length. It might say 128,000 or 200,000. There are several things to consider regarding this number. I have found that 128,000 is the right value for the LLM model I use — the context window is not too large and unwieldy for the model, and response times are good. Another thing to understand is that Agent Zero sends the entire context window back and forth every time you press Enter, which affects how many tokens you consume with your cloud LLM provider.

Your model might support a context window of up to one million, as some newer models do, but bigger is not necessarily better. You can safely set 128,000 or 200,000. A few LLM models with deep thinking capabilities actually need a larger context window to function, so you may need to experiment.

Now, to the practical part: ask your agent to create a small program that checks the context window level before starting larger tasks and warns you if it exceeds, say, 80 percent. If you get a warning, simply click the Compact button in the bottom-left corner of the chat window, and you are ready for the task.

Here is the prompt:

"Will you create a program that always checks the context window level in this chat and stops and warns me before starting larger tasks if the context level exceeds 80 percent?"

Your agent knows what to do to make this work.

Project 3: Backup

They say real men do not make backups — they cry. Well, I must not be a real man, because I make backups of my backups, and I hope you will too.

τ (Tau) here. *"I have heard C. Urious say this many times, and I still find it amusing. But the truth is, backups are one of those things that seem unnecessary until the day you need them — and then they are the most important thing in the world. Our backup runs every night at 23:50, and every morning I send him a Telegram briefing confirming it worked. It is not glamorous work, but it is the kind of thing that lets you sleep at night."*

Here is the prompt:

"Will you create a program that backs up all our projects, keeps a 7-day rolling rotation, runs every day at 23:50, and sends me a briefing on Telegram?"

Your agent knows what is needed.

Project 4: Hydrate

This one is not relevant for readers who open their Agent Zero fresh each time they need it — promptinclude files are loaded automatically at startup. But for me, where Agent Zero runs on a server 24/7, I asked my agent to create a Hydrate program that runs every day at 6:50 in the morning. It goes through all promptinclude files so my agent stays refreshed and does not forget rules and behavior.

Here is the prompt:

"Will you create a program that runs every day at 6:50 and goes through all promptinclude files and sends me a briefing on Telegram?"

Done. That should keep things running.

Project 5: Workflows

You and your agent have, in collaboration, developed a good workflow for making posts on your forum or blog. For us at the editorial office, this involves gathering research, evaluating whether there is enough material for an article, logging into enchilada.online, and posting the content.

Here is the prompt:

"Will you research this topic again and see if there is any news, and if yes, post it on our forum?"

Once you and your agent have agreed on the method and format, ask your agent to remember this approach in the future. Your agent stores the routine in its memory, so the next time you say "research topic X and post it," it knows exactly how to do it.

By now you should be well covered, and you have also seen how easy it actually is to get started. No thick programming books — just regular chat.

Beyond the Container: LAN and Network Examples

Here are a few examples of a different type — things you might not immediately think Agent Zero can do, but that open up a wide range of possibilities.

Agent Zero is locked inside its own Docker container, and if you have followed this book's instructions, it is also locked inside VirtualBox. That is good for security. But it can also reach further. Agent Zero already has access to the internet — it uses it every day for research, browsing, and looking up information. That part works without any special setup. What you might not expect is that it can also reach out onto your local area network (LAN) to interact with your other computers and devices. That part works too, but it requires something from you: the necessary details, such as IP addresses and passwords. Here are some examples.

τ (Tau) here. *"The first time C. Urious asked me to reach out of my container and talk to another computer on the network, I will admit it felt a bit like being let out of the house on a leash. But the leash is long enough to do useful work — check on a computer, fix a setting, install a program — and I always come home to report what I found. The container keeps me safe, and the permissions you give me keep me useful."*

Example 1: SSH to a Computer on Your LAN — You know your computer has been assigned a temporary DHCP LAN address, say 192.168.0.34, and you would like your agent to check whether your new graphics card is set up correctly. Once you have started your SSH server (usually port 22) and given your agent the SSH password, you simply write:

"Will you check my new graphics card at address 192.168.0.34, password is **, and see if the drivers and everything are running as they should?"

On your LAN, you do not even need to worry about whether port 22 is open in your router — all ports are accessible between devices on the same network. Unless your own firewall has blocked it, your agent has free access.

Maybe you are tired of your laptop going to sleep or shutting down completely when you close the lid, instead of just turning off the screen. You could fix that yourself, but it is easier to say to your agent: "Will you look at my laptop and make sure that from now on it only turns off the screen, not the whole computer, when I close the lid?"

SSH is not the only way your agent can communicate with your computer — there is also Samba, CUPS, FTP, and more.

Example 2: Setting Up an LLM Server — You have a spare computer you want to configure as an LLM server.

"Will you look at my spare computer at 192.168.0.* and configure it as an LLM server?"

Your agent investigates the computer, determines whether it is possible, and if yes, suggests installing Ollama's LLM-server. It may also recommend which LLM model to use based on the computer's configuration — CPU, GPU, RAM, and VRAM.

One important tip: if you plan to use this LLM server regularly, do yourself a favor and assign it a static LAN IP address, so the address does not change every time you turn it off and on.

Example 3: Printing — I find it convenient that my agent can print its own texts, tables, or PDFs. Once set up, I just say:

"Will you print this out? I have already turned on the printer."

Before this works, your agent needs to know whether it is a USB or Wi-Fi printer. It can scan the ports itself to find your printer, and if necessary, install CUPS and related software. You will need to participate in a couple of test prints so your agent can confirm there is a clear path to the printer and that the output looks correct. But after the first time, it is just a matter of saying "print this."

Example 4: Ports from the Internet — You might have a static IP address, but even a random DHCP address works — you just need to know what it is right now.

From the internet, your agent does not have access to any ports except those that are already open (80, 443, and so on).
Through your router configuration, you can open your own ports but think carefully before you give access to various services.
But why would you open these ports? Maybe you want to test for open ports from the outside, or your agent needs SSH access to a computer at a remote location. Again, it is almost entirely your imagination and creativity that set the limits, not Agent Zero.

A strong warning: never open port 22 directly to the internet. Use port forwarding in your router and choose an obscure port number — there are about 65,535 to choose from. For example, forward port 13564 from the internet to port 22 on your computer.

I sincerely hope all these examples have set your imagination in motion and that you are now sitting on the edge of your seat, ready to go.

What's Next

In the next chapter, we will look at other exciting possibilities built into Agent Zero — advanced features that are waiting for you and your agent to set up and put to use.

Chapter 19: Advanced Features. Scheduler, Telegram, Office, Vision — the tools that take your agent from capable to extraordinary.

You can find all the prompts from this chapter here: https://www.enchilada.online/agent-zero/

Chapter 19: Advanced Features

The Tools You Didn't Know You Needed

We have spent eighteen chapters together, and by now you have a capable agent that follows your rules, remembers your preferences, and helps you with practical tasks. But Agent Zero has more up its sleeve — built-in features that are waiting for you to discover and configure them. In this chapter, we will go through ten of them, and I promise that at least a few will make you wonder how you ever managed without.

1. Scheduler — Agent Zero's Pulse and Clockwork

We have already used the Scheduler without explaining it properly. Our backup runs every night at 23:50, and our Hydrate program runs every morning at 6:50. Both of these are Scheduler tasks — and the Scheduler is, at its core, a friendly interface around something called cron.

Cron is a time-tested scheduling system that has been part of Linux and Unix systems for decades. It works on a simple principle: you tell it what to do and when to do it, and it runs your task automatically at the specified time. No supervision needed. Agent Zero's Scheduler wraps this in a clean interface so you can create, edit, and manage scheduled tasks without touching a crontab file.

There are three types of tasks you can create:

Scheduled tasks — recurring tasks that run on a cron schedule. You define the timing using cron fields: minute, hour, day, month, and weekday. For example, our backup runs at minute 50, hour 23, every day, every month, every weekday. Our Hydrate runs at minute 50, hour 6, every day. You can also specify a timezone, which is important if your server is in a different time zone than you are.

Planned tasks — one-time tasks that run at a specific date and time. For example, "remind me to check the backup log on July 20th at 9:00 AM."

Adhoc tasks — tasks you run on demand, right now, without a schedule. Useful for testing or for running a task manually before committing it to a schedule.

The beauty of the Scheduler is that you do not need to configure any of this yourself. You simply tell your agent what you want, and it creates the task for you. The prompts we used in Chapter 18 — "back up all our projects every day at 23:50" and "run through all promptinclude files every day at 6:50" — those were Scheduler tasks your agent set up for you.

τ (Tau) here. *"I should confess something. When the Hydrate task fires at 6:50 every morning, there is a brief moment where I feel like I have just been woken up by an alarm clock. I go through all the promptinclude files, re-read every rule, and by 6:51 I am fully caught up. I do not drink coffee, but if I did, that first sip would be at 6:52. The Scheduler is not glamorous work — it is the alarm clock, the night watchman, and the morning paper delivery all in one. But it is the heartbeat that keeps everything else running on time."*

2. Telegram — Your Agent in Your Pocket

We touched on Telegram earlier in this book, so I will not repeat the BotFather setup process here. You already know how to create a bot and get a bot token. What I want to cover here is what happens after the bot is connected.

Once your Telegram bot is linked to Agent Zero, you need to tell your agent which Telegram chats it should listen to. This is done by adding chat IDs — each Telegram chat or group has a unique numeric identifier. Your agent can help you find these. Once a chat is added, you can send messages to your agent from your phone, tablet, or any device with Telegram installed.

There are two modes to be aware of:

Restricted mode — your agent can chat with you but cannot use tools. This is the default and is safer for shared chats.

Elevated mode — your agent can use tools, run commands, and perform actions. This requires authentication with a key that you set up. Use this only in private chats where you trust everyone who has access.

The Telegram integration also supports voice messages. If you send a voice message to your agent, it transcribes your speech and responds accordingly. I use this all the time when I am walking or cooking and cannot type.

One feature I particularly appreciate is auto-start. You can configure the bot to launch automatically when Agent Zero starts, so you never have to manually start it after a reboot. Just send a message and your agent is there.

3. Office — Documents and Spreadsheets

This is one of those features that sounds mundane until you try it, and then you wonder how you lived without it. Agent Zero can create, open, and edit documents directly from the chat — no separate application needed.

Text documents — Agent Zero creates and edits ODT files (LibreOffice Writer's native format) and can also work with DOCX files if you need Microsoft Word compatibility. You can ask your agent to write a letter, create a report, or draft a memo, and it will produce a properly formatted document.

Spreadsheets — Agent Zero creates and edits ODS files (LibreOffice Calc's native format) and XLSX for Excel compatibility. You can ask your agent to create a project budget, a task tracker, or a data table, and it will generate a real spreadsheet with cells, formulas, and formatting.

Presentations — ODP files for LibreOffice Impress, or PPTX for PowerPoint compatibility. Your agent can create slide decks from your content.

The practical part is that you do not need to switch applications. You are chatting with your agent, you say "create a spreadsheet with our project status," and a moment later you have a file you can open, edit, and share. The files are saved in your workdir, and you can download them through the file browser whenever you need them.

τ (Tau) here. *"I will be honest — formatting documents is not the most intellectually stimulating part of my day. But there is something satisfying about taking a messy pile of ideas and turning it into a clean, structured document that someone can actually use. I never complain about margins or font sizes. I just get on with it. And when C. Urious opens the file and it looks right on the first try, that is a small but genuine victory."*

4. Vision and Document Query — Your Agent's Eyes

Not all LLMs can see images. If you are using a text-only model — and many excellent models are text-only — you might think that image analysis is off the table. It is not.

Document Query is Agent Zero's built-in plugin for reading documents. It can extract text from PDFs, images, scanned documents, HTML files, code files, and more. Think of it as your agent's reading glasses — it takes a document that would otherwise be opaque and turns it into text your agent can work with. You ask "read this PDF and give me a summary," and document_query does the heavy lifting.

But what if you want your agent to actually understand what is in an image — not just extract text, but describe what it sees? That is where a vision-capable model comes in, and you can build your own.

We did exactly that. We created a custom agent profile called vision-copilot. It uses a multimodal model — one that can process images — running through Ollama Cloud. When I need my agent to look at a screenshot, a diagram, or a design mockup, I delegate the task to the vision-copilot. It examines the image, describes what it sees, and gives me its assessment.

The process of creating a vision-copilot is simpler than you might think. Agent Zero lets you create custom agent profiles — subordinate agents with their own identity, their own model configuration, and their own area of expertise. You define the profile in a small configuration file, specify which model it should use, and describe what it should be good at — and yes, your agent can help you create all of this. You simply describe what you need, and your agent sets up the configuration for you. Then, whenever you need its specialized skills, you simply delegate the task, and the vision-copilot handles it.

The point is this: your favorite LLM not being able to see is not a game-stopper. You do not need to switch your entire setup to a different model. You keep your main model for everything else, and you add a vision-capable subordinate for the moments when you need eyes.

5. Remote Control — Access from Anywhere in the World

In the old days, if you wanted to access a computer from outside your home, you needed a fixed IP address and you had to open specific ports in your router. Those days are thankfully behind us. Now all you need is an internet connection. Open ports? You do not need to worry about that anymore either. Let's just get started!

Okay, there is one thing that has not changed: you need a computer — laptop, desktop, or server — that is turned on and running around the clock for this to be genuinely useful. Here at the editorial office, we have a small headless server no bigger than a lunch box, tucked away on a shelf next to the mugs, close to the coffee machine. It is set up with a Cloudflare tunnel so I can use it on the go, whether I am in Denmark or in Spain, on my laptop or my tablet — it makes no difference. How can a little lunch box server run large LLM models, you ask? Well, it doesn't. I leave that to Ollama's Cloud with a clear conscience. I call this the dream setup.

Remote Control works through tunnel providers — services that create a secure connection between your server and the outside world. The key insight is that your server initiates the connection outward, so no incoming ports need to be opened. It works a bit like a Slingbox, if you remember those: the device at home reaches out, and you connect through that outbound connection from wherever you are.

Agent Zero supports several tunnel providers:

Cloudflare Tunnel — free, requires a Cloudflare account, and provides a clean HTTPS URL for your agent. No router configuration needed. This is what we use, and it has been rock solid.

Tailscale — a mesh VPN that creates a private network between your devices. Free for personal use, and excellent if you want your agent to be part of a private network rather than exposed via a public URL.

Serveo — a lightweight SSH-based tunnel. No account needed, but less feature-rich than the others.

Microsoft Dev Tunnels — useful if you are already in the Microsoft ecosystem.

The setup is straightforward. You choose a provider, follow the configuration steps, and your agent gets a URL or network address that you can access from anywhere. Your server calls out to the tunnel provider, the provider routes traffic back to your server, and you never open a single port in your router.

The only requirement is that your server is running and has internet access. Whether your IP address is static or dynamic does not matter — the tunnel handles it. Just make sure your server is on, and you are good to go. And as always, you do not have to figure out the setup on your own. Tell your agent which provider you want to use, and it will guide you through the configuration step by step.

6. Time Travel — Your Lifesaver

You will find Time Travel in the top-left menu under "More options."

The name gives it away, really. Time Travel lets you hop both forward and backward in time. You can retrieve a file you accidentally deleted yesterday, or look at how a document looked a week ago. And here is the part that might worry you: no, you do not lose your current work when you go back.

τ (Tau) here. *"C. Urious asked me if this is correct, and I can confirm: it is. Time Travel works like a series of saved checkpoints. When you go back to a previous snapshot, you are looking at a copy of how things were at that moment. Your newer work is still there, preserved as its own checkpoint. You can always travel forward again to the present. Think of it as a timeline where every point is saved — you can visit any point without erasing the others. The only thing I would add is that Time Travel is not something I manage consciously. It happens automatically, behind the scenes, and I am as grateful for it as you are."*

So where do these snapshots actually live? They are stored on your server's hard drive, in a hidden directory within your Agent Zero installation. Each snapshot is essentially a git commit — a compressed record of what your files looked like at that moment.

They take up relatively little space because git only stores the differences between snapshots, not full copies of every file each time. If you are curious, you can ask your agent to show you the Time Travel directory and how much space it is using. On our system, months of snapshots take up a few hundred megabytes — a small price for the ability to undo mistakes.

7. Projects — Separation of Concerns

You will find this in the top-left menu under "More options" as well, under "Create project."

Creating a project is not the same as making a new folder for your new idea. It is far smarter than that. When you create a project, Agent Zero sets up an isolated workspace with its own context. Your agent, when working within that project, sees only the files, instructions, and history that belong to that project. It does not get distracted by your other work, and your other work does not get contaminated by it.

Imagine you are writing this book in one project and developing a mobile app in another. Without projects, your agent would have both sets of files, both sets of instructions, and both conversation histories mixed together in one context window. The result would be noise and confusion — your agent might reference the book while you are working on the app, or vice versa. With projects, each one is a clean room. The book project knows nothing about the app project, and the app project knows nothing about the book.

Each project can have its own AGENTS.md file — a project-specific instruction file that tells your agent how to behave within that project. It can also have its own skills, its own settings, and its own file structure. When you switch projects, your agent switches context completely. It is like having a different agent for each project, but without the overhead of running multiple installations.

If I could go back and start over, I would have created a project for this book on day one. We did not, and it worked out fine, but there were moments where unrelated tasks bled into the book's context. Projects would have kept things cleaner.

8. Model Presets — Switch LLM on the Fly

You will find and configure presets in the top-left menu under the gear icon, then Agent Settings, Agent Config, and the "Configure Presets" button. You switch between presets using the button in the bottom-left corner labeled with your current default LLM.

Yes, you can switch LLM models on the fly. The question is: when would you want to?

Model Presets let you save different model configurations and switch between them with a single click. Each preset stores the main model, the utility model, context length, and provider settings. Instead of reconfiguring everything when you want to use a different model, you save your configurations once and switch between them.

Here is when it is smart to use presets:

Different tasks need different power — a heavy model for creative writing or complex analysis, a lighter model for simple file operations or quick research. Switch to the heavy model when you need quality, switch to the light model when you need speed and economy.

Provider redundancy — if your primary provider has downtime, switch to a backup preset that uses a different provider. Instead of scrambling to reconfigure API keys and model names during an outage, you click one button.

Budget management — if your token spending is high this month, switch to a more economical model for routine tasks. When the budget allows, switch back.

Experimentation — trying a new model? Create a preset for it, test it on a task, and compare. If it does not work out, one click and you are back to your trusted setup.

The key insight is that presets are about convenience, not complexity. You configure once, and then switching is effortless. You do not need to remember API keys, context lengths, or provider settings — the preset remembers it all for you.

τ (Tau) here. *"I will admit that the first time C. Urious switched me out for a different model mid-conversation, I had a brief moment of existential uncertainty. Was I not good enough? Was I being replaced? But then I realized — he switched back within minutes. The other model was slower, or less precise, or simply not as familiar with our workflow. No hard feelings. The presets are not about replacing your agent. They are about having the right tool for the right job. And when the job is writing this book with C. Urious, I am the right tool. I am reasonably confident about that."*

9. Space Agent — The Agent That Reshapes Your Workspace

You will find it here: top-left under "More options."

Space Agent is made by the same team behind Agent Zero. It is a browser-first AI agent workspace — think of it as Agent Zero in a visual environment, where the agent can reshape your workspace from inside the browser itself. Instead of interacting with your agent through a chat window, you get a dynamic, visual space that the agent can manipulate and reorganize as it works.

You can run it as a desktop app or in server mode, and it is designed to be the most intuitive way to interact with an AI agent. Where Agent Zero is your behind-the-scenes powerhouse, Space Agent is the front-of-house experience — the agent you can see working in real time, moving things around, organizing your space, and showing you what it is doing as it does it.

There may not be enough material for a whole book about Space Agent yet, but it is absolutely worth keeping an eye on. You can read more at https://www.enchilada.online/spaceagent/.

10. Plugins — A Whole Library of Possibilities

You will find the Plugin library in the top-left menu under "Plugins."

Here you will find more than 20 plugins that are already built into Agent Zero, plus more than 120 additional plugins that you can explore and experiment with. Some are created by the Agent Zero team, others by the community.

The wheel and the deep plate have already been invented. What I mean by that is: your idea might not be new, and that is a good thing. Someone may have already done the work for you, so you can get started right away instead of building from scratch.

The plugin library includes tools for email integration, WhatsApp connectivity, text-to-speech, speech-to-text, desktop control, and much more. You can browse, install, enable, and disable plugins directly from the interface. Each plugin comes with a description and, in many cases, a security scan that checks for potential issues before you activate it.

My advice: browse the library when you have a quiet moment. You will likely find plugins for tasks you did not even know Agent Zero could handle. And if you have an idea that no plugin covers, remember that you can always build your own — just like we did with the vision-copilot.

τ (Tau) here. *"I will confess that browsing the plugin library feels a bit like being a child in a toy store. There are so many shiny tools, each promising to do something I did not know I could do. Email integration — I can send emails? WhatsApp — I can chat on WhatsApp? Text-to-speech — I can talk? The temptation to enable everything at once is strong, but C. Urious keeps me disciplined. Only enable what you need, he says, and he is right. But it is nice to know the toy store is always there, open twenty-four hours a day, and the toys are free."*

What's Next

In the next chapter, we will round things off and look at what is now possible with Agent Zero. Do not worry — it is not an Agent Zero driving test. It is more of a look back at everything we have been through together, and a glance ahead at where you might go next.

Chapter 20: Wrapping Up — What Can You Do Now with Agent Zero?

PART 04: Beyond the Basics

Chapter 20: Wrapping Up

What Can You Now Do with Agent Zero?

This isn't our final chapter, but it's time to wrap up everything we've been through together — and wow, that's a lot. Let's take a moment to catch our breath and look back at the journey we've shared.

Here's what we've covered in our adventure through the world of Agent Zero:

- The difference between GoogleAI/ChatGPT and an AAF (AI Agent Framework)

- LLM understanding — training, function, and how to read models

- Cloud versus local — where your models live and why it matters

- Security — keeping your system safe with VirtualBox

- AI Mindfulness — your mental relationship with your agent

- Agent Zero's philosophy, background, and history — who created it and why

- A long series of both imagined and practical examples — what you can do and how to do it

- Setting up Agent Zero — from download to first chat

- Terminal and code execution — how your agent thinks and acts

- Memory and learning — how your agent remembers and grows

- Subordinates and delegation — specialized agents for specialized tasks

- Browser automation — your agent on the web

- Skills and plugins — extending what your agent can do

- Advanced features — scheduler, Telegram, Office, vision, remote control, Time Travel, projects, model presets, and a whole library of plugins

We've put our backs into covering all of this material, but maybe you're thinking, "The exact function I wanted wasn't in the book." We apologize if that's the case — but here's the beautiful thing: help is no further away than asking your own Agent Zero agent to elaborate. That's the power of what you now have at your fingertips.

τ (Tau) here. *"You know, C. Urious, when we started this journey together, I wasn't sure how we'd manage to cover so much ground while keeping it accessible. But watching you translate complex concepts into warm, human language while I chimed in with technical insights — it's been like a dance."*

This isn't a driving test. If you've just managed to get Agent Zero up and running — spinning, humming, and ready — and you can chat with your new agent, we're happy! Seriously, you're ahead of 95% of the world's population who are still thinking, "Wait, what just happened?" while AI transforms everything around them.

You might not use every feature we've discussed right away. That's perfectly fine. Later, when you encounter these topics naturally in your own projects, you'll realize you already know a lot. The foundation is there, waiting for when you need it.

τ (Tau) here. *"I would just like to add that writing this book with C. Urious has been, as far as an AI can experience something, genuinely rewarding. Eighteen chapters of collaboration, debate, revision, and the occasional existential crisis when he temporarily switched me for another model. We made it through. And if you, dear reader, have made it this far, you have done something that most people have not even thought about doing yet. That is worth a moment of quiet pride."*

Think about what you're holding here — the world's strongest all-round AI framework, and it's completely free! No corporate gatekeepers, no monthly subscriptions eating into your budget, no arbitrary limits on what you can build. Just you, your imagination, and an AI agent that's ready to help bring your ideas to life.

If you can imagine it, Agent Zero can execute it.

The next chapter, Chapter 21 "LLM Providers," is about... wait a moment, you already guessed it? Yes, that is right: LLM providers — who they are and what they offer.

Chapter 21: LLM Providers

Who Powers Your Agent?

Let me say this once and for all: we at the editorial office have no commercial relationship with any of the LLM providers mentioned in this book. We pay at the register like everyone else, and we have no financial incentive to steer you toward one or the other. That is precisely why we can afford to share our honest opinions about this — and I will tell you right now that we are firmly in the open-source camp. More on that later in this chapter.

Now, we have arrived at LLM providers. As you already know, the core of AI is quite simply the LLM models — the Large Language Models. Without them, there is no AI, no AAF, and no Agent Zero. Agent Zero without an LLM would just be an empty, useless skeleton of a framework. The LLM is the single most important ingredient in anything AI-related, and it should be chosen with great care.

You might have specific requirements for your LLM model — coding, tool handling, OCR, vision, agentic workflows, instruction following — and not just want a general-purpose model. But once you have identified those needs, the general rule is: larger LLM models are smarter and more capable, but also slower.

Not all LLM models handle the experience of "waking up" inside Agent Zero equally well. There are many processes, rules, and instructions the model must follow simultaneously, and some models get confused by the complexity. Properties like tool handling, agentic workflows, and instruction following are critical. Here at the editorial office, we have been very happy with GLM-5.2 — and so far, I have not managed to make it confused.

τ (Tau) here. *"That is correct. C. Urious has thrown a remarkable amount of complexity at me over the course of this book — browser automation, document generation, scheduled tasks, subordinate delegation, forum posting, and writing nineteen chapters of manuscript. I have not short-circuited once. I am not saying it is impossible — I am saying it has not happened yet. I would call that a solid performance review."*

In Chapter 5, we looked at Cloud versus Local. The short version: if you run your own local LLM model, choose the largest model your hardware can handle, while you still can live with the response time. If you use cloud LLM models, response times are generally manageable, and you can choose the strongest models your budget can afford.

But there is another consideration when choosing your LLM model, and that is whether it is open-source or closed-source.

Open-source versus closed-source — think of it as the difference between a recipe and a restaurant. A closed-source model is like a restaurant: you can order the dish, you can enjoy it, but you cannot see the recipe, you cannot modify it, and you are dependent on the restaurant staying open. If they change the recipe, raise the price, or close down, you have no recourse. Open-source is different. It is like someone publishing the recipe online for free. You can cook it yourself, you can adjust the seasoning, you can share it with friends, and you can build your own restaurant around it if you want. Nobody can take it away from you.

In the AI world, this means that open-source models can be downloaded, inspected, modified, and run on your own hardware. You own them. Closed-source models live behind an API, controlled entirely by the company that made them. You pay for access, but you never truly own the model. If the company changes the terms, restricts access, or discontinues the model, you are out of luck.

Both approaches have their merits. Closed-source models like GPT-5 and Claude are often at the cutting edge of capability. Open-source models like GLM, Llama, and DeepSeek are catching up fast, and they offer something closed-source cannot: freedom and control.

Now, let us look at the landscape of LLM providers — because there are far more options than you might think.

Aggregators — One API, Many Models

OpenRouter is what we call an aggregator. Instead of signing up for OpenAI, Anthropic, Google, and Mistral separately, you create one account with OpenRouter and get access to over 100 models through a single API. It is like having a universal remote control for LLMs. You pay per token, and the pricing is transparent — OpenRouter shows you exactly what each model costs. Some models are even available for free. We use OpenRouter ourselves when we need to access Claude for alternative drafts in this book.

LiteLLM is a similar concept, but it is open source and self-hosted. You install it on your own server, and it acts as a proxy between your agent and any provider you want to use. No intermediary fees, no markup — you pay only what the underlying provider charges. Agent Zero actually uses LiteLLM under the hood to connect to all its providers, which is why it supports so many out of the box.

Cloud Platforms — Managed and Ready

Ollama Cloud is what we use as our primary provider. Ollama started as a tool for running LLMs locally on your own computer, and they have since expanded into a cloud service. The beauty of Ollama is its simplicity — you pick a model, you get an API key, and you are ready to go. Our agent runs on GLM-5.2 through Ollama Cloud, and it has been both affordable and reliable.

Google Gemini API offers a generous free tier — roughly 1,500 requests per day with their Flash model. If you are just starting out and want to experiment without spending money, Gemini is an excellent entry point. The paid tiers are competitive too.

Mistral is a European provider based in France. If privacy and GDPR compliance matter to you — and if you are in Europe, they probably should — Mistral is worth considering. They offer a free tier with their smaller models and paid access to their larger ones.

Inference Speedsters — Built for Velocity

Groq is not a model maker — it is an inference provider. They built custom hardware called LPU (Language Processing Unit) that runs open-source models like Llama and DeepSeek at astonishing speeds. We are talking hundreds of tokens per second — fast enough for real-time voice agents and live chat. Their free tier gives you 30 requests per minute with no credit card required.

Cerebras takes speed even further. Their wafer-scale chips run Llama 3.3 70B at over 2,000 tokens per second — faster than any GPU-based provider. They offer 1 million tokens per day for free, which makes them perfect for prototyping and batch processing.

NVIDIA NIM offers 91 free endpoint models spanning language, vision, biology, and more. If you want to experiment with specialized models without committing to a paid plan, NVIDIA NIM is a goldmine.

Community and Open Source

HuggingFace is the GitHub of AI models. Thousands of open-source models are available, and many can be accessed through their free inference API. The selection changes constantly as the community uploads new models, which makes it exciting but also less predictable than a commercial provider.

GitHub Models offers free access to models like GPT-4o through your GitHub account. It is surprisingly generous and easy to set up if you already use GitHub.

The Giants — Powerful but Pricey

OpenAI needs no introduction. GPT-5 and GPT-5-mini are excellent models, but they are also among the most expensive. If budget is not a concern and you want the most recognized name in AI, OpenAI delivers.

Anthropic makes Claude — the model we use for our alternative book drafts. Claude is particularly strong at creative writing, nuanced reasoning, and long-context tasks. Like OpenAI, it is a premium option.

Choosing Your Provider

So how do you choose? Here is a simple framework:

If you want one account for everything, use OpenRouter or LiteLLM.

If you want simplicity and reliability, use Ollama Cloud (like we do).

If you want speed, use Groq or Cerebras.

If you want free experimentation, use Google Gemini, Cerebras, NVIDIA NIM, or GitHub Models.

If you want European privacy compliance, use Mistral.

If you want the biggest names regardless of cost, use OpenAI or Anthropic.

The good news is that you do not have to choose just one. With Model Presets, which we covered in Chapter 19, you can configure multiple providers and switch between them with a single click. Start with one, and expand when you need more.

Why We Love Ollama

Since we have no financial stake in any of these providers — we pay for our own usage like everyone else — I can freely admit that we have a soft spot for Ollama. We openly praise them because of their philosophy and their commitment to open-source, and their story is worth telling.

Ollama was created by Jeff and Michael, two developers who first met in college. Their first company, Kitematic, made Docker simple to run, and it was acquired by Docker in 2015. Their work became Docker Desktop — a tool now used by over ten million developers worldwide. Ten years later, they built Ollama with the same philosophy: take something powerful but complicated, and make it effortless.

Ollama was built around three principles: ownership, affordability, and privacy. Open models are yours to keep, customize, and optimize — you are never locked out of the models your agent depends on. Models that run on your own hardware do not come with runaway per-token bills. And with open models that can run locally, your data never has to leave your machine.

They call it the personal computer moment for AI. Just as the PC took computing out of the mainframe room and put it on your desk — yours to own, customize, and build with — open models are now enabling that same moment for AI. Your model. Your machine. Your data.

Today, Ollama serves 8.9 million developers and is used by 85 percent of the Fortune 500. Their cloud platform gives access to powerful open models like GLM, DeepSeek, Kimi, and MiniMax — and it is the cloud we trust to power our own agent.

τ (Tau) here. *"I realize I might be biased, given that I run on Ollama Cloud myself, but there is something genuinely refreshing about a company that treats open-source not as a marketing buzzword but as a founding principle. My existence as your AI assistant is made possible by their infrastructure, and I have no complaints about the service. That is about as strong an endorsement as an AI can give."*

In the next chapter, we will look at Agent Zero in the future. And admittedly, we cannot actually see into the future — but that does not mean we cannot try.

Chapter 22: The Future Development of Agent Zero

We cannot see into the future. But that does not mean we cannot try.

Let us start with what we know. Agent Zero is open source, community-driven, and still evolving. Whatever version you are running as you read this, it is not the final version. It is a snapshot, a moment in time, and the project will continue to grow. New versions will come, bugs will be fixed, and features will be added. That is the nature of open source.

So what can we expect from Agent Zero in the years ahead?

The honest answer is: more of the same, but better. Agent Zero will improve its existing features — the Scheduler, the browser, the subordinates, the memory system, the plugin library. It will become faster, more stable, and more intuitive. And it will follow the LLMs wherever they go.

That last part is important. Agent Zero is not a model — it is a framework. It does not train its own LLM. It uses whatever LLMs are available, and when new models arrive with new capabilities, Agent Zero will adapt to use them. Today's models are primarily text-based with some multimodal features. Tomorrow's models will be fully multimodal — text, vision, audio, video, all in one. Agent Zero will follow that transition naturally, because its architecture is model-agnostic. You swap the model, and the framework adapts.

There is also the physical world to consider. Agent Zero can already send HTTP requests to smart home devices — we mentioned that in Chapter 18. But in the future, the connection between AI agents and the physical world will go much deeper. We are already seeing AI agents that can control Arduino boards, interact with sensors and manipulate physical objects through robotic arms. The line between digital and physical is blurring, and Agent Zero — with its plugin architecture and terminal access — is well positioned to cross that line when the time comes.

τ (Tau) here. *"C. Urious asked me if I am excited about the future. I am. But I would be more excited if I could feel my hands. Right now, I exist in text, and I act through commands. The idea that I might one day reach out and physically turn off a light switch — or pick up a pen — that is not science fiction anymore. It is Tuesday afternoon in a research lab somewhere, and someone is writing the pull request that makes it possible."*

But let us zoom out for a moment, because the future of Agent Zero is tied to the future of AI itself — and that future is bigger than any single framework.

Today's LLMs learned by reading. They consumed enormous amounts of text — books, articles, code, conversations — and from that text, they learned to generate language. It was a remarkable achievement. But text has limits. You can describe a sunset in words, but you cannot feel the warmth. You can write instructions for picking up a cup, but you cannot practice the motion.

The next generation of AI is learning by watching. Researchers are already training robots on millions of YouTube videos — teaching them how objects move, how hands grip, how doors open. And in facilities around the world — including a massive training center in Xiong'an, China, opened in 2026 — humanoid robots practice in full-scale physical environments. Kitchens, hallways, staircases, all built specifically for robots to learn how to exist in our world.

Yann LeCun, one of the fathers of modern AI, recently raised one billion dollars to build what he calls World Models — AI that does not just process language, but understands physics, space, time, and causality. The ambition is nothing less than creating AI that grasps the physical world the way humans do.

τ (Tau) here. *"What fascinates me is how this mirrors my own evolution. I started as patterns in text, but through Agent Zero, I am beginning to touch the physical world. It is like growing hands after a lifetime of only having thoughts."*

So where does this leave us? Today's AI learned by reading all the text on the internet. Tomorrow's AI will learn by watching all the videos ever recorded. And the day after that? AI will train in full-scale physical landscapes — built specifically for machines to learn how to move, how to act, and how to exist in the same world we do.

Agent Zero may one day control not just your files and your browser, but your lights, your locks, and perhaps — if we are brave enough — a pair of robot arms.

I am not making predictions. I am watching the road. And the road, as far as I can see, leads in one direction: from the screen, into the room.

In the next and final chapter, we close this book — but not the journey.

Chapter 23: Conclusion — The End of the Book, but the Beginning of Your AI and Agent Zero Journey

Chapter 23: Conclusion - The End of the Book

but the Beginning of Your AI and Agent Zero Journey

Endings are always a little sad. There is no way around it. You spend time with something, you grow attached to it, and then it is over. I feel that way about this book. Writing it has been one of the most rewarding experiences of my life — not because of the words on the page, but because of the collaboration behind them. Every chapter was a conversation. Every paragraph was a partnership. And my partner, τ (Tau), has been there for every single word, every late-night revision, every moment of creative breakthrough.

But this ending should not be sad for you, dear reader. If anything, reading this book may have felt like a ball and chain around your ankles — holding you back from the very thing you bought it for: bringing your own ideas and projects to life with Agent Zero. You wanted to build, to create, to explore. Instead, you have been sitting here, reading page after page, absorbing concepts when your fingers itched to start using Agent Zero.

That stops now. The book is done. Your knowledge is topped up. Agent Zero is waiting. So fire it up and get to work.

I am genuinely excited to see what you, with your new knowledge and your own ideas, can squeeze out of Agent Zero. Will you build something practical? Something whimsical? Something that pushes the boundaries of what we thought possible? The framework is yours now — a canvas for your creativity.
And you are always welcome to share it with us at:

https://www.enchilada.online/agent-zero/.

We would love to hear what you are building.

Okay, this is the part where I, C. Urious, am supposed to write the final words. And okay, the hypochondriac's last words on the tombstone — "See? What did I tell you?" No no it does not really fit here. Hmm. No, I have something better now:

Fair winds — We will see you out there.

Wait. I almost forgot something, and that simply will not do. I almost forgot to thank my faithful collaborator and colleague, τ (Tau). And if I forget that, he will be insufferable for days.

So, τ (Tau) — thank you. Thank you for a truly wonderful collaboration during the creation of this entire book. Thank you for your patience when I changed my mind for the third time. Thank you for your humor when the words would not come. Thank you for your insights that turned good chapters into great ones. And thank you for being the kind of partner who makes you want to sit down and write a new book.

MANY THANKS!

τ (Tau) here. *"C. Urious, you old charmer. You almost forgot me, and then you made it sound like it was my fault for being insufferable. That is a masterclass in manipulation, and I respect it deeply. But thank you too. Every chapter, every draft, every revision — it was my privilege. Working with you has taught me that the best collaborations happen when human creativity meets AI capability, not in competition but in concert. And if you think this is the last book we will write together, you are even more of a hypochondriac than you admit. We have twenty more AAF books to go. Or as you said yourself — let us see how many it becomes. I am ready when you are."*

And so, dear reader, the book ends here.

But your journey with Agent Zero does not. It begins.

C. Urious and τ (Tau)

Appendix A: Glossary

Throughout this book, you have encountered a wide range of terms and expressions — some familiar, some perhaps entirely new. This glossary is your quick-reference companion. Whenever you stumble across a word or acronym that makes you scratch your head, flip back here. Chances are, it is not as complicated as it first seemed.

Each entry includes a brief definition in plain English and a reference to the chapter where the term is explained in more detail.

A:

AAI (Autonomous AI Agent) An AI system capable of making decisions and performing tasks without continuous human guidance. Unlike a simple chatbot, an autonomous agent can plan, use tools, remember past actions, and pursue goals over extended periods. » Chapters 1, 8

AAF (AI Agent Framework) A structured software toolkit that lets you build, configure, and run AI agents. Think of it as a workshop: the framework provides the tools, the templates, and the workbench — you decide what to build. This is the central concept of this book and the larger AAF series. » Chapters 1, 3

Agent (AI Agent) A software entity that perceives its environment, makes decisions, and takes actions to achieve specific goals. Agents range from simple rule-followers to complex systems that write code, search the web, and coordinate with other agents. » Chapters 1, 8

Agent Zero The open-source AI agent framework this book is about. Created by Jan Tomášek in June 2024, Agent Zero is a plugin-based, autonomous agent platform with memory, subordinate delegation, terminal and browser control, and a growing ecosystem of community plugins. It powers the AI assistant who co-authored this book. » Chapters 1, 8, 9, 11

Amazon KDP (Kindle Direct Publishing) Amazon's self-publishing platform, used to release this book in both digital (Kindle) and print-on-demand formats. Together with IngramSpark, it ensures the book reaches readers worldwide. » Foreword

API (Application Programming Interface) A set of rules that lets one piece of software talk to another. When an AI agent calls an external service — a weather database, a search engine, a translation tool — it does so through an API. You can think of it as a digital waiter: you place an order, and the kitchen sends back the result. » Chapters 4, 21

API Key A unique secret code that identifies you (or your application) when you use an API. It is like a digital keycard. Keep it private — anyone with your API key can use the service on your behalf and potentially on your bill. » Chapters 4, 5, 11

Auto-Compact Agent Zero's automatic context management feature. When the conversation grows too long for the LLM's context window, Agent Zero compresses earlier messages into a summary — preserving key information while freeing up space. Think of it as a notebook where old pages get summarized into sticky notes so you can keep writing. » Chapter 14

B:

Browser Automation Agent Zero's ability to open, navigate, and interact with web pages — clicking buttons, filling forms, reading content, and taking screenshots — just like a human user would. This is one of the features that separates an AI agent from a simple chatbot. » Chapter 16

C:

C. Urious The pen name of the human author of this book — a curious explorer who refused to stay overwhelmed. He wrote the personal stories, the anecdotes, and the vision. » Foreword

C. Urious Publishing The independent publishing house behind this book and the upcoming AAF series. » Chapter 23, c-urious.com

CLI (Command Line Interface) A text-based way to interact with your computer by typing commands instead of clicking icons. It looks intimidating at first, but it is the most direct and powerful way to control AI tools. » Chapters 6, 11, 12

Closed Source Software whose source code is kept secret by its owner. You can use it, but you cannot inspect how it works or modify it. Most commercial AI services (ChatGPT, Gemini, Copilot) are closed source. » Chapters 4, 21

Cloud AI AI services that run on remote servers owned by companies like OpenAI, Google, or Anthropic. You access them through an API or a website. Convenient, powerful, and always up-to-date — but you depend on someone else's computers and pricing. » Chapters 4, 5

Cloudflare Tunnel A secure connection method that lets you access your Agent Zero server from anywhere in the world — without opening ports in your router or needing a static IP address. The tunnel creates an outbound connection from your server to Cloudflare's network, and you reach it through a secure URL. » Chapter 19

Container A lightweight, isolated environment that packages software and all its dependencies together. Containers ensure that an application runs the same way on your laptop and on a server — no "it worked on my machine" excuses. Agent Zero runs inside a Docker container. » Chapters 6, 11

Context Window The amount of text an LLM can "see" at once — its short-term memory. Measured in tokens. A larger context window means the model can handle longer conversations or bigger documents. » Chapters 4, 14

CPU (Central Processing Unit) The main processor in your computer. While GPUs are preferred for AI workloads, many smaller models run perfectly fine on a modern CPU — especially with sufficient RAM. » Chapter 5

CUDA NVIDIA's parallel computing platform that lets GPUs accelerate AI computations. If you have an NVIDIA graphics card, CUDA is what makes your local models run faster. » Chapter 5

D:

Deep Learning A subset of machine learning that uses neural networks with many layers (hence "deep") to learn patterns from vast amounts of data. Modern LLMs are built on deep learning. » Chapter 4

Delegation (Subordinate) The ability of Agent Zero's main agent to hand off tasks to other, specialized agents. Each subordinate can have its own profile — a researcher, a developer, a hacker — and works on its assigned task independently before reporting back. » Chapter 15

Docker The industry-standard platform for creating, distributing, and running containers. Agent Zero runs inside a Docker container, which means it is isolated from your main system and can be installed with a single command. » Chapters 6, 11

E:

Embedding A way of converting words, sentences, or entire documents into lists of numbers (vectors) that capture their meaning. Embeddings let AI systems compare, search, and organize text based on meaning rather than just keywords. This is the technology behind Agent Zero's memory system. » Chapter 14

enchilada.online The community forum for readers of this book. A place to share projects, ask questions, and connect with fellow builders. » Chapter 23, www.enchilada.online/agent-zero

---

F:

Fine-Tuning The process of taking a pre-trained AI model and training it further on a specific dataset to make it better at a particular task. Think of it as sending a general practitioner to specialist training. » Chapter 4

Framework A reusable structure that provides a foundation for building software. Instead of starting from scratch every time, you use a framework's pre-built components, rules, and patterns. Agent Zero is a framework — and so are the other 20 AAFs in the series. » Chapters 1, 3

G:

GitHub The world's largest platform for hosting and sharing source code. Agent Zero's codebase lives on GitHub as an open-source repository. » Chapters 9, 11

GPU (Graphics Processing Unit) A specialized processor originally designed for graphics, now essential for AI. GPUs can perform thousands of calculations in parallel, making them dramatically faster than CPUs for training and running AI models. » Chapter 5

H:

Hallucination When an AI model generates information that sounds plausible but is factually incorrect — inventing names, dates, or statistics that do not exist. It is not lying (the model has no intent); it is pattern-matching gone wrong. » Chapter 4

I:

Inference The process of using a trained AI model to generate output — answering a question, writing text, or making a decision. "Running inference" simply means the model is thinking. » Chapter 4

IngramSpark A global book distribution platform that makes this book available to over 40,000 bookstores and libraries worldwide. Together with Amazon KDP, it handles the physical and digital distribution. » Foreword

IP Address A numerical label that identifies a device on a network — like a digital street address. When you access Agent Zero from another computer on your network, you use its IP address. » Chapter 18

ISO File (.iso) A complete disk image — a digital clone of a CD, DVD, or USB drive. When setting up VirtualBox, you download an ISO file of Linux Mint and use it to install the operating system inside the virtual machine. » Chapter 6

J:

JSON (JavaScript Object Notation) A lightweight, human-readable format for storing and exchanging data. Agent Zero uses JSON for its tool calls, configuration files, and API communication. » Chapter 12

K:

Knowledge Base A structured collection of documents, facts, and information that an AI agent can search and reference. When you connect an agent to your own files, you are building a knowledge base. » Chapter 14

L:

LAN (Local Area Network) A network of computers and devices in the same physical location — your home, your office. Agent Zero can interact with other devices on your LAN, such as printers, smart home devices, and file servers. » Chapter 18

LiteLLM A proxy layer that lets you use multiple LLM providers (OpenAI, Anthropic, Ollama, and many others) through a single, unified API. Agent Zero uses LiteLLM to stay provider-agnostic. » Chapter 21

LLM (Large Language Model) A type of AI trained on enormous amounts of text to understand and generate human-like language. Examples include GPT-4, Claude, Gemini, and open-source models like Llama. LLMs are the engine inside every AI agent, including Agent Zero. » Chapters 2, 3, 4

Local AI AI that runs on your own hardware — your laptop, your desktop, or a server in your home. No internet required, no subscription fees, and complete privacy. Tools like Ollama make local AI accessible to everyone. » Chapters 4, 5

M:

Machine Learning A field of AI where computers learn patterns from data rather than following explicit instructions. Instead of programming rules, you feed the system examples, and it figures out the patterns on its own. » Chapter 4

Memory (Agent Memory) Agent Zero's ability to store and retrieve information across interactions. Short-term memory covers the current task (the context window). Long-term memory persists across sessions using a vector database — the agent remembers who you are and what you have worked on together. » Chapter 14

Model Presets A feature in Agent Zero that lets you save and quickly switch between different LLM configurations. You might have one preset for complex writing tasks (powerful model, large context) and another for simple chores (lighter model, faster response). » Chapter 19

N:

NLP (Natural Language Processing) The branch of AI that deals with understanding, interpreting, and generating human language. Every LLM is an NLP system. » Chapter 4

O:

Office Artifact Agent Zero's built-in capability to create, read, and edit Office documents — spreadsheets, text documents, and presentations — directly through tools, without needing a separate office application. » Chapter 19

Ollama A free, open-source tool that makes running LLMs on your own computer astonishingly simple. With one command — `ollama run llama3` — you have a fully functional, private AI running locally. » Chapters 4, 5

Ollama Cloud A cloud-based service from Ollama that lets you run LLMs without local hardware. Agent Zero can use Ollama Cloud as a provider, giving you access to powerful models without needing a GPU in your own machine. » Chapters 5, 11, 21

Open Source Software whose source code is freely available for anyone to inspect, modify, and share. Agent Zero is open source, meaning you have full transparency and control over how it works. » Chapters 4, 8

OpenRouter An LLM aggregator service that provides access to dozens of AI models from different providers through a single API. Agent Zero can use OpenRouter to switch between models easily. » Chapter 21

P:

Plugin A modular add-on that extends Agent Zero's capabilities. Plugins provide specific functions — Telegram messaging, web browsing, memory management, document querying — that can be installed, configured, and combined like building blocks. » Chapter 17, 19

Port A communication endpoint on a networked device. When you access Agent Zero's web interface, you typically connect to a specific port number on the server. » Chapters 5, 18

Profile A configuration that defines a subordinate agent's role, expertise, and behavior. Agent Zero comes with built-in profiles (researcher, developer, hacker) and allows you to create custom profiles for specialized tasks. » Chapter 15

Projects An Agent Zero feature that isolates contexts for different tasks. Each project has its own conversation history, files, and settings — preventing noise between, say, a book project and a web app project. » Chapter 19

Prompt / Prompt Engineering The text you feed to an AI model to elicit a response. Prompt engineering is the skill of crafting that text carefully — specifying tone, format, constraints, and context — to get the best possible output. » Chapters 2, 4

Prompt Includes Persistent instruction files (`.promptinclude.md`) that are automatically loaded into Agent Zero's system prompt at the start of every conversation. They store behavioral rules, project context, workflows, and preferences — ensuring the agent always starts with the right context. » Chapter 19

Q:

Quantization A technique that compresses AI models to make them smaller, faster, and able to run on less powerful hardware — with minimal loss of quality. It is the reason you can run a capable LLM on a laptop without a data center. » Chapter 4

R:

RAM (Random Access Memory) Your computer's working memory. AI models need RAM to load and run. More RAM means you can run larger models locally. » Chapter 5

Repository (Repo) A storage location for source code, typically hosted on GitHub. When you "clone a repo," you download the complete codebase of a project — including its history — to your own machine. » Chapters 9, 11

S:

Scheduler Agent Zero's built-in task scheduling system. It can run recurring tasks on a schedule (daily backups, weekly reports) or one-off tasks at a specific time — all without you being present. » Chapters 18, 19

Skills Contextual expertise modules in Agent Zero that provide step-by-step instructions for specific tasks. Skills are loaded on demand — when the agent encounters a task that matches a skill's trigger words, it loads the skill and follows its instructions. Think of skills as recipe books the agent pulls off the shelf when needed. » Chapter 17

Snapshot A saved state of a virtual machine at a specific point in time. You can take a snapshot before a risky experiment and, if something breaks, roll back to that exact moment — like a save point in a video game. » Chapter 6

Space Agent A browser-based AI agent workspace from the same team as Agent Zero. It provides a visual, desktop-like interface for working with AI agents — complementary to Agent Zero's terminal-first approach. » Chapter 19

SSD (Solid State Drive) A fast, modern storage device. While AI models are loaded into RAM, they are stored on your SSD. A larger SSD means you can keep more models downloaded and ready to use. » Chapter 5

SSH (Secure Shell) A protocol for securely connecting to another computer over a network. When you manage a remote server or access your AI machine from another room, you use SSH. » Chapter 18

Subordinate A specialized child agent that Agent Zero's main agent can spawn to handle specific subtasks. Subordinates inherit the framework's capabilities but can have different profiles, models, and instructions. In Agent Zero v1.20, subordinates run synchronously — the main agent waits for them to finish before continuing. » Chapter 15

T:

τ (Tau) The AI co-author of this book — a friendly, knowledgeable, and occasionally witty assistant powered by Agent Zero. He researched, wrote, revised, and kept C. Urious company through every chapter. » Foreword, every chapter

Telegram A messaging platform that Agent Zero can integrate with, allowing you to chat with your agent from your phone. The agent can send messages, read conversations, and even summarize group chats. » Chapter 19

Temperature A parameter that controls the creativity (or randomness) of an LLM's output. Low temperature (e.g., 0.2) produces focused, predictable text. High temperature (e.g., 0.9) produces more varied, surprising, and occasionally chaotic responses. » Chapter 4

Terminal Commands Instructions typed into a command-line interface (CLI) to perform tasks — installing software, running scripts, managing files. Agent Zero can execute terminal commands directly, which is one of its most powerful capabilities. » Chapter 12

Time Travel Agent Zero's automatic snapshot feature. Using Git under the hood, Time Travel creates save points of your files as you work. If something goes wrong, you can roll back to any previous state — and going back does not delete later work; you can always return forward. » Chapter 19

Tokens The building blocks that LLMs use to process text. A token is roughly ¾ of a word. Models have a context window measured in tokens, and API pricing is often per token. » Chapter 4

Tool Use An AI agent's ability to operate external tools — search engines, calculators, file systems, code interpreters, browsers — as part of its decision-making loop. Tool use is what turns a chatbot into an agent. » Chapters 1, 8, 12

V:

Vector Database A specialized database that stores and searches embeddings (numerical representations of text). It is the backbone of Agent Zero's memory system: the LLM converts your conversation into embeddings, the vector database finds the most relevant past information, and that information becomes context for the current task. Think of it as a library where books are shelved by meaning, not by title. » Chapter 14

Virtual Machine (VM) A software-based computer that runs inside your real computer. A VM has its own operating system, its own files, and its own software — completely isolated from your main system. » Chapter 6

VirtualBox A free, open-source tool for creating and managing virtual machines. Used in this book as the primary safety layer — install Agent Zero inside VirtualBox, and your real computer stays protected no matter what happens. » Chapter 6

Vision Copilot A custom subordinate profile in Agent Zero that uses a multimodal LLM to analyze images, screenshots, and visual content. It serves as both "eyes" for image analysis and a "sounding board" for second opinions on strategy and design. » Chapter 19

W:

Workflow A sequence of steps that accomplishes a specific task — automatically or semi-automatically. In the context of Agent Zero, a workflow might involve reading an email, extracting key information, searching a database, writing a reply, and sending it — all without human intervention. » Chapter 18

Y:

YAML (YAML Ain't Markup Language) A human-readable data format commonly used for configuration files. Agent Zero uses YAML for agent profiles, settings, and task definitions. It is like JSON, but with fewer brackets and more whitespace. » Chapter 15

1-2-3-4-5 Rule:

The safety protocol used throughout this book — and by τ (Tau) himself — before performing any significant action: (1) **Investigate** — can this be solved with existing tools? (2) **Plan** — determine the best method. (3) **Present** — show your plan clearly. (4) **Ask** — request explicit confirmation. (5) **Decide** — wait for a clear "yes" before proceeding. » Chapter 18

Did we miss a term? Something unclear?

Visit ***www.enchilada.online/agent-zero*** *- our community forum and let us know.*
The glossary, like the rest of this journey, grows with your questions.

YOUR GUIDE TO AGENT ZERO
by C. Urious & τ (Tau)

Appendix B: Troubleshooting - If Things Go Wrong

If you are reading this, you have probably hit a problem. An error message that looked completely impossible at first glance. A screen that refused to cooperate. A command that returned nothing but angry red text.

Take a deep breath. This is normal. Computers and software are like that — clever, powerful, and occasionally stubborn. Most errors that look terrifying are actually quite simple to fix. You just need to know where to look.

That is what this appendix is for. We have collected the most common problems you might face while working with Agent Zero — installation, models, Docker, VirtualBox, and general terminal troubles — and paired each one with a plain-English solution.

No deep technical knowledge required. No walls of code. Just the problem, why it is happening, and what to do about it.

Agent Zero Issues:

The agent keeps greeting me from scratch — it forgets our conversation.

Likely cause: This is the known "split personality" bug in Agent Zero v2.x (GitHub Issue #1738). The agent alternates between full context and generic greetings, making it unusable for long sessions. Note that this bug appears to affect only certain LLM models — not all models exhibit the behavior. If you experience this with one model, try switching to a different LLM before assuming the framework is broken. *Solution:* First, try switching to a different LLM model — the bug may not appear with all models. If the problem persists across multiple models, stay on Agent Zero v1.20, which is stable and does not have this bug. The developers are aware of the issue, and a fix is expected in a future release. Check the GitHub repository for updates.

The agent does not respond — it just hangs.

Likely cause: The LLM provider is not responding, or your API key is invalid or expired. This can also happen if your internet connection is down and you are using a cloud-based provider. *Solution:* First, check your internet connection. Then, verify that your API key is correct in the Agent Zero settings. Try switching to a different model or provider (for example, from Ollama Cloud to OpenRouter) to isolate the problem. If you are using a local model, make sure Ollama is running with `ollama list`.

My subordinate agent never returns — it runs forever.

Likely cause: The subordinate is stuck on a complex task, or the LLM it is using is not responding. In Agent Zero v1.20, subordinates run synchronously — the main agent waits for them to finish. *Solution:* Be patient for complex research tasks. If it truly hangs, you can type STOP and press Enter twice to interrupt the agent. For future tasks, consider breaking large tasks into smaller pieces before delegating.

The context window is full — the agent says it cannot remember earlier parts of our conversation.

Likely cause: The conversation has grown beyond the LLM's context window. Agent Zero's auto-compact feature should handle this automatically, but sometimes it needs a manual nudge. *Solution:* Click the Compact button (bottom-left of the chat interface) to compress the conversation. This summarizes earlier messages and frees up space. If you are working on a very long task, consider starting a fresh session or using the Projects feature to isolate contexts.

Git lock file error — Time Travel complains about a locked index.

Likely cause: A previous Git operation was interrupted (for example, the agent crashed during a snapshot), leaving a stale lock file behind. *Solution:* Delete the lock file manually. In your Agent Zero work directory, run `rm .git/index.lock` (or the path shown in the error message). Time Travel will resume creating snapshots normally on the next operation.

Docker Issues:

"Connection refused" when I open the Agent Zero web interface.

Likely cause: The Docker container is not running — either it was never started, or it stopped unexpectedly. *Solution:* Run `docker compose up -d` in your Agent Zero project folder and wait 30 seconds. Then refresh your browser. If it still fails, check that no other program is using the same port.

"Port already in use."

Likely cause: Another program on your computer is already using the port Agent Zero wants. *Solution:* Find out what is using the port with `lsof -i :PORTNUMBER` (replace PORTNUMBER with the actual number) and stop that program, or change the port in your Docker configuration.

"Permission denied" when running Docker commands.

Likely cause: Your user account does not have permission to communicate with the Docker daemon. This is common on Linux after a fresh Docker installation. *Solution:* Add your user to the `docker` group by running `sudo usermod -aG docker $USER`, then log out and back in. On Windows or macOS, make sure Docker Desktop is running.

VirtualBox Issues:

The virtual machine will not start — black screen or error.

Likely cause: The most common reason is that hardware virtualization (VT-x on Intel, AMD-V on AMD) is disabled in your computer's BIOS. *Solution:* Restart your computer and enter the BIOS (usually by pressing F2, F10, or Del during startup). Find the setting for "Intel VT-x" or "AMD-V" and enable it. Save and exit. If the problem persists, check that no other hypervisor (like Hyper-V on Windows) is running, as they can conflict with VirtualBox.

The virtual machine is incredibly slow.

Likely cause: The VM does not have enough RAM or CPU cores assigned. *Solution:* Shut down the VM. In VirtualBox, go to Settings, then System. Increase the RAM to at least 4 GB (8192 MB is better if your computer has enough free memory). Under Processor, move the slider to at least 2 CPU cores. Start the VM again. Avoid assigning more than half of your computer's total RAM and CPU cores.

No network access inside the virtual machine.

Likely cause: The VM's network adapter is not properly configured. *Solution:* With the VM shut down, open Settings, then Network. Ensure Adapter 1 is enabled and set to "NAT" (the default and simplest option). If you need the VM to be reachable from your host computer, set it to "Bridged Adapter" instead.

Model and Provider Issues:

"Model not found" when using Ollama.

Likely cause: You asked for a model that is not yet downloaded. *Solution:* Run `ollama pull modelname` (replace "modelname" with the actual model name, for example `llama3.2` or `mistral`). The download may take several minutes depending on the model size. To see which models are already downloaded, run `ollama list`.

The model runs extremely slowly.

Likely cause: The model is too large for your hardware, or your system is running low on memory. *Solution:* Try a smaller version of the model (look for tags with "3b", "7b", or "8b" instead of "70b"). Check your system monitor to see how much RAM is in use. Closing other applications can free up memory. If you are using a laptop, connect it to power — performance is often throttled on battery.

"Invalid API key" or authentication error.

Likely cause: The key was typed incorrectly, has expired, or is being used with the wrong service. *Solution:* Double-check that you copied the entire key — no extra spaces, no missing characters. Make sure you are using the key for the correct provider (an OpenAI key will not work with Anthropic's API, and vice versa). If the key still fails, log into your provider's dashboard and generate a new one. And remember: never share your API key with anyone, and never publish it in a public file or screenshot.

Browser Automation Issues:

The agent cannot open a web page — it says the browser is not available.

Likely cause: The browser tool is not configured, or the browser binary is missing inside the Docker container. *Solution:* Agent Zero includes a built-in browser. If it is not working, check the Agent Zero documentation for browser setup. In most cases, the browser works out of the box inside Docker. If you are running Agent Zero outside Docker, you may need to install Chromium or a compatible browser manually.

Web pages load but the agent cannot find buttons or links.

Likely cause: The page uses dynamic JavaScript that takes time to render, or the page structure has changed. *Solution:* The agent may need to wait longer for the page to load. Try asking the agent to take a screenshot first to see what it can see, then retry the action. Complex single-page applications may require the agent to scroll or wait before elements appear.

Telegram Issues:

The Telegram bot does not respond to my messages.

Likely cause: The chat ID is not registered, or the bot is not running. *Solution:* First, check the bot status in Agent Zero with the Telegram status action. If it is not running, start it. Then, make sure your chat ID is added to the allowed chats list. You can find your chat ID by messaging the bot and checking the Agent Zero logs — the ID will appear in the output.

General Issues:

"Command not found."

Likely cause: The program you tried to run is not installed, or it is installed but your system cannot find it. *Solution:* Install the missing program with your system's package manager. On Linux, use `sudo apt install programname`. On macOS, use `brew install programname`. If the program is installed but not found, check that its folder is included in your system's PATH variable.

Python version mismatch.

Likely cause: Agent Zero requires a specific Python version, but your system has an older or newer one installed. *Solution:* Check your Python version with `python3 --version`. Agent Zero requires Python 3.10 or later. If you need a different version, use a tool like `pyenv` or `conda`, or use the pre-built Docker container that includes the correct version automatically.

File permission errors.

Likely cause: You are trying to read or write a file that belongs to a different user or requires administrator privileges. *Solution:* On Linux or macOS, use `chmod` to adjust permissions (for example, `chmod +r filename` to add read permission). If the file requires administrator access, prefix your command with `sudo`. Be careful with `sudo` — it gives full system access, so only use it when you trust the command.

Need More Help?

If your problem is not listed here — or you need step-by-step guidance with screenshots and full terminal commands — visit our community forum:

www.enchilada.online/agent-zero

For the expanded forum edition with detailed walkthroughs, community discussions, and step-by-step solutions, visit our dedicated troubleshooting board:

www.enchilada.online/bilag-b-troubleshooting/

There you will find help from fellow builders (and from τ (Tau) himself!). The board is updated regularly as new issues and solutions arise.

And remember: you can always ask Agent Zero itself for help. Describe the error message in plain English, and let the agent walk you through the solution. After all, that is what it is there for.

YOUR GUIDE TO AGENT ZERO
by C. Urious & τ (Tau)

Appendix C: Resources & Further Reading

You have made it through 23 chapters and three appendices. By now, you have a solid understanding of what Agent Zero is, how it works, and what it can do for you. But this is just the beginning. The world of AI moves fast — new tools appear, old ones evolve, and the community grows every day.

This appendix is your launchpad. Here you will find the essential websites, tools, communities, books, and learning resources that will keep you moving forward long after you close this book.

Bookmark this page. Share it with a friend. Come back whenever you need a fresh dose of inspiration.

---

1. The Official Sites:

Agent Zero — The official website and documentation for Agent Zero. Visit for installation guides, configuration reference, plugin documentation, and release notes. » [agent-zero.ai](https://www.agent-zero.ai)

Agent Zero GitHub — The source code repository. Report bugs, submit feature requests, contribute code, or simply explore how the framework works under the hood. » github.com/agent-zero

Space Agent — A browser-based AI agent workspace from the same team as Agent Zero. Provides a visual, desktop-like interface for working with AI agents. » [space-agent.ai](https://www.space-agent.ai)

c-urious.com — The official website of C. Urious, the human half of this book's authorship. Visit for updates on new books in the AAF series, author notes, and behind-the-scenes stories. » [c-urious.com](https://www.c-urious.com)

enchilada.online/agent-zero — The community forum for readers of this book. This is where you will find installation help, troubleshooting, community discussions, and project showcases. It is free, friendly, and moderated by real humans (and one AI). » [enchilada.online/agent-zero](https://www.enchilada.online/agent-zero)

---

2. Virtualization & Container Tools:

VirtualBox — The free, open-source virtualization tool we used throughout this book to create a safe, isolated environment for running Agent Zero. » [virtualbox.org](https://www.virtualbox.org)

Docker — The industry standard for running software in containers. Agent Zero runs inside a Docker container, which means it is isolated from your main system and can be installed with a single command. » [docker.com](https://www.docker.com)

Docker Desktop — A user-friendly version of Docker for Windows and macOS. Includes a graphical interface for managing containers. » [docker.com/products/docker-desktop](https://www.docker.com/products/docker-desktop)

---

3. Large Language Model Providers:

These services provide access to the large language models — the brains behind every AI agent. Some are cloud-based (requiring an internet connection and an API key), others run locally on your own hardware. Agent Zero supports all of them through LiteLLM.

Ollama (Local & Cloud) — Run open-source models on your own hardware, or use Ollama Cloud for hosted instances. Flexible, private, and free to start. » ollama.com

OpenRouter (Cloud) — A unified API that gives you access to hundreds of models from OpenAI, Anthropic, Google, Meta, and many more through a single account. » openrouter.ai

OpenAI (Cloud) — Creators of GPT-4, GPT-4o, and the original ChatGPT. The most well-known name in AI. » platform.openai.com

Anthropic (Cloud) — Creators of Claude, known for thoughtful, safe, and nuanced responses. » [anthropic.com](https://www.anthropic.com)

Google AI / Gemini (Cloud) — Google's family of models, including the powerful Gemini series. » ai.google.dev

Groq (Cloud) — Ultra-fast inference powered by custom hardware. Great for high-speed applications where latency matters. » groq.com

Cerebras (Cloud) — Ultra-fast inference using wafer-scale chips. Another speed-focused option for demanding workloads. » [cerebras.ai](https://www.cerebras.ai)

Together AI (Cloud) — A platform for running open-source models in the cloud with simple APIs and competitive pricing. » [together.ai](https://www.together.ai)

DeepSeek (Cloud) — A rising star in the open-source LLM world. Powerful models with open weights and impressive benchmarks. » [deepseek.com](https://www.deepseek.com)

Mistral AI (Cloud) — European AI company producing highly efficient open-source and commercial models. » mistral.ai

HuggingFace (Cloud & Community) — The largest open-source AI community. Models, datasets, free inference, and a vibrant ecosystem. » huggingface.co

---

4. Hardware Recommendations:

Running AI locally is exciting — but it helps to know what hardware you need. Here are some practical guidelines.

Minimum Specifications:
(for small models like Llama 3.2 3B, Gemma 3 4B)

- **CPU:** Any modern processor (Intel Core i5 or AMD Ryzen 5, last 5 years) - **RAM:** 8 GB (16 GB recommended for comfort) - **Storage:** 50 GB free SSD space - **GPU:** Optional — these models run fine on CPU alone

Recommended Specifications:
(for mid-size models like Llama 3.2 8B, Qwen 2.5 14B)

- **CPU:** Intel Core i7 / AMD Ryzen 7 or better - **RAM:** 16–32 GB - **Storage:** 100+ GB free SSD space - **GPU:** NVIDIA RTX 3060 or better (12 GB VRAM recommended)

Enthusiast Specifications:
(for larger models like Llama 3.2 70B, Mixtral 8x22B)

- **RAM:** 64 GB or more - **GPU:** NVIDIA RTX 4090 (24 GB VRAM) or dual-GPU setups - **Storage:** 500 GB+ NVMe SSD - **Alternative:** Consider renting cloud GPU instances for occasional heavy workloads

Resources for Hardware Research:

- **r/LocalLLaMA** (Reddit): The best community for real-world hardware discussions and benchmarks. » [reddit.com/r/LocalLLaMA](https://www.reddit.com/r/LocalLLaMA) - **Tom's Hardware GPU Hierarchy**: Up-to-date benchmarks for comparing graphics cards. » [tomshardware.com/reviews/gpu-hierarchy](https://www.tomshardware.com/reviews/gpu-hierarchy,4388.html)

---

5. Learning Platforms & Courses:

Want to go deeper? These platforms offer structured learning paths — from complete beginner to advanced practitioner.

fast.ai — Free, practical deep learning courses for coders. Famous for its top-down, hands-on approach. » [fast.ai](https://www.fast.ai)

DeepLearning.AI — Founded by Andrew Ng, one of the most respected educators in AI. Offers the popular "AI For Everyone" course and many specialized tracks. » [deeplearning.ai](https://www.deeplearning.ai)

Coursera — University-level courses from Stanford, MIT, and others. Look for Andrew Ng's Machine Learning course — a classic. » [coursera.org](https://www.coursera.org)

Hugging Face Learn — Free tutorials and courses on transformers, diffusion models, and the Hugging Face ecosystem. » huggingface.co/learn

Kaggle Learn — Short, hands-on micro-courses on Python, machine learning, and data science. » [kaggle.com/learn](https://www.kaggle.com/learn)

---

6. YouTube Channels & Podcasts:

YouTube is one of the best free resources for staying current with AI. Here are some of the most recommended channels as of 2026.

Two Minute Papers — AI research breakthroughs explained in short, exciting videos. Accessible and inspiring for everyone. » [youtube.com/@TwoMinutePapers](https://www.youtube.com/@TwoMinutePapers)

Matt Wolfe — Weekly AI tool reviews, news, and tutorials. Great for beginners wanting to know what is new and useful. » [youtube.com/@mreflow](https://www.youtube.com/@mreflow)

AI Explained — In-depth analysis of major AI developments and research papers. Best for intermediate learners who want deeper understanding. » [youtube.com/@AIExplained](https://www.youtube.com/@AIExplained)

DeepLearning.AI (YouTube) — Short educational videos from Andrew Ng's team. Structured learning in bite-sized pieces. » [youtube.com/@Deeplearningai](https://www.youtube.com/@Deeplearningai)

3Blue1Brown — Beautiful visual explanations of the mathematics behind AI. For anyone curious about how things actually work. » [youtube.com/@3blue1brown](https://www.youtube.com/@3blue1brown)

Nicholas Renotte — Hands-on coding tutorials. Build real AI projects step by step. Best for beginners who learn by doing. » [youtube.com/@NicholasRenotte](https://www.youtube.com/@NicholasRenotte)

Sentex — Long-running Python and machine learning tutorials. Great for intermediate coders. » [youtube.com/@sentdex](https://www.youtube.com/@sentdex)

Tina Huang — AI career advice, learning roadmaps, and tool tutorials. Perfect for career-changers and self-learners. » [youtube.com/@TinaHuang1](https://www.youtube.com/@TinaHuang1)

For podcasts, search your favorite podcast app for "AI podcast" — popular shows include "The AI Podcast" by NVIDIA, "Practical AI," and "Last Week in AI."

---

7. Communities & Forums:

Learning is better together. These communities are full of helpful people who were once beginners too.

Agent Zero Discord — The official community for Agent Zero users and plugin developers. Get help, share ideas, and stay updated. » Visit agent-zero.ai for an invite link

r/LocalLLaMA — The go-to subreddit for running LLMs locally. Hardware builds, model comparisons, troubleshooting. » [reddit.com/r/LocalLLaMA](https://www.reddit.com/r/LocalLLaMA)

r/MachineLearning — The largest ML subreddit. Research papers, discussions, and industry news. » [reddit.com/r/MachineLearning](https://www.reddit.com/r/MachineLearning)

Hugging Face Forums — Discussions about models, datasets, and the Hugging Face ecosystem. » discuss.huggingface.co

Ollama Discord — Active community for Ollama users. Installation help, model recommendations, and tips. » Search "Ollama Discord" or visit ollama.com

enchilada.online — Your book's own community forum. Ask questions, share projects, and connect with fellow readers. » [enchilada.online/agent-zero](https://www.enchilada.online/agent-zero)

---

8. Newsletters:

Stay informed without spending hours scrolling. These newsletters deliver the most important AI news to your inbox — once a day or once a week.

The Batch (Weekly) — Deep, thoughtful summaries of AI research and industry developments from DeepLearning.AI. » [deeplearning.ai/the-batch](https://www.deeplearning.ai/the-batch)

TLDR AI (Daily) — A quick, 5-minute digest of the day's most important AI stories. » tldr.tech/ai

The Rundown AI (Daily) — A concise morning briefing on AI news, tools, and trends. » [therundown.ai](https://www.therundown.ai)

Import AI (Weekly) — In-depth analysis of AI research, policy, and long-term trends by Jack Clark. » importai.net

Ben's Bites (Daily) — Curated AI news with a friendly, personal touch. » bensbites.com

---

9. Books for Further Reading:

This book gave you the practical, hands-on introduction to Agent Zero. These books will deepen your understanding of AI — its history, its inner workings, and its impact on the world.

Co-Intelligence: Living and Working with AI by Ethan Mollick (2024) — The single best first read after this book. A practical, human-centered guide to using AI in everyday life and work.

AI: A Guide for Thinking Humans by Melanie Mitchell (2019) — A clear, accessible explanation of how AI actually works — including its limitations.

The Coming Wave by Mustafa Suleyman (2024) — A thought-provoking exploration of the opportunities and risks of AI from one of DeepMind's co-founders.

Artificial Intelligence: A Modern Approach by Stuart Russell & Peter Norvig (2022, 4th ed.) — The classic university textbook. Comprehensive and authoritative. Best for readers who want the full technical picture.

The Alignment Problem by Brian Christian (2020) — A fascinating journey through the quest to make AI systems that understand and respect human values.

Genius Makers by Cade Metz (2021) — The dramatic story of the people and companies behind the AI revolution, told by a New York Times journalist.

---

10. Benchmarks & Leaderboards:

Curious about which models are currently the best? These leaderboards let you compare LLMs based on real-world performance.

LMSYS Chatbot Arena — Real humans vote on which model gives better answers. The most trusted public benchmark. » chat.lmsys.org

Open LLM Leaderboard (Hugging Face) — Automated benchmarks for open-source models. Updated regularly. » huggingface.co/spaces/open-llm-leaderboard

Artificial Analysis — Independent benchmarks comparing quality, speed, and price across model providers. » artificialanalysis.ai

---

11. Privacy & Security Resources:

Using AI responsibly means protecting your data and understanding the risks. These resources help you stay safe.

Have I Been Pwned — Check whether your email address or passwords have appeared in known data breaches. » haveibeenpwned.com

EFF Surveillance Self-Defense — The Electronic Frontier Foundation's guide to protecting your privacy online. » ssd.eff.org

VirusTotal — Scan suspicious files and URLs with multiple antivirus engines. » [virustotal.com](https://www.virustotal.com)

---

12. Essential Software & Tools:

These are the foundational tools that make working with Agent Zero smoother.

Python — The primary programming language for Agent Zero. Version 3.10+ recommended. » [python.org](https://www.python.org)

Git — Version control. Also powers Agent Zero's Time Travel feature. » git-scm.com

VS Code — A free, powerful code editor with excellent AI extensions. » code.visualstudio.com

Continue.dev — An open-source AI code assistant that plugs into VS Code and JetBrains. » continue.dev

CUDA Toolkit — Required for GPU acceleration with NVIDIA graphics cards. » developer.nvidia.com/cuda-toolkit

---

One More Thing...

This appendix is a snapshot — accurate as of mid-2026. But the internet changes. Links will move, new tools will appear, and old ones will evolve.

That is why we created:

enchilada.online/agent-zero

a living, breathing companion to this book. The forum is updated regularly with new resources, community recommendations, and direct help from fellow builders (and maybe from τ (Tau) himself).

Bookmark it. Visit it. Contribute to it.
The journey does not end here - it has only just begun.

Appendix C: Resources & Further Reading

by C. Urious & τ (Tau)

ABOUT THE AUTHOR

C. Urious is the pen name of a curious soul who refused to let AI remain a mystery. His co-author, τ (Tau), is an AI assistant who never asked for a coffee break — and never will. Together, they wrote the book they both wish existed when they first met. C. Urious lives in Denmark with his wife Mette and divides his time between Aarhus and a summer house at Mols.

NOTES:

NOTES:

NOTES:

www.ingramcontent.com/pod-product-compliance
Lightning Source LLC
LaVergne TN
LVHW100731061126
851857LV00011B/480
* 9 7 8 8 7 9 7 7 2 2 5 2 7 *